6.95

THE HUNTING OF THE BUFFALO

The Hunting of the Buffalo

E. DOUGLAS BRANCH

UNIVERSITY OF NEBRASKA PRESS · *Lincoln and London*

International Standard Book Number 0–8032–5021–5

First Bison Book printing April, 1962

Most recent printing shown by first digit below:
7   8   9   10

Bison   Book   edition   reprinted   by   arrangement   with
Appleton-Century-Crofts,   Inc.

E. DOUGLAS BRANCH, SINGULARISIMO

BY J. FRANK DOBIE

> *I like odd characters. I am one.*—BALZAC
> *How glorious it is—and also how pain-*
> *ful—to be an exception.*—DE MUSSET

Edward Douglas Branch was born in Houston, Texas, July 7, 1905; he had a younger brother and two sisters. The family was of Methodist persuasion, although I never heard him express any interest in any church, and certainly after he got away from home he never entered one to worship. For that matter, I never heard him even allude to his father, whom he resembled closely in both physical and intellectual qualities. The founder of the Branch family in Texas came from Virginia in 1833, fought in the Battle of San Jacinto, was elected to the first

---

*Several individuals have contributed biographical data for this sketch, which must remain personal. They include Paul Angle, Chicago Historical Society; Hartman Dignowity, Blacksburg, Virginia; John T. Frederick, Notre Dame University; John Hakac, University of Arizona; Jim Dan Hill, Wisconsin State College, Superior; W. Ross Livingston, State University of Iowa, Iowa City; Franklin J. Meine, Chicago; William J. Petersen, The State Historical Society of Iowa; Kendall B. Taft, Roosevelt University; Walker D. Wyman, Wisconsin State College, River Falls.

Congress of the Republic of Texas, and then became a member of the Republic's Supreme Court. Edward Thomas (commonly called Tom) Branch, Douglas' father, began working in a bookstore at the age of twelve and "devoured the stock day and night." A fragile, little man, he read law, had a prodigious memory, became one of the most distinguished members of the Texas bar, recodified the criminal laws of the state, wrote law books and—without monetary compensation—saw Branch's *Annotated Penal Code* (Chicago, 1916) become the Bible of criminal courts and trial lawyers throughout Texas. Revised and enlarged in 1956, it remains "the Bible."

After graduating from a Houston high school, Douglas entered the University of Texas in January of 1922. He was a sophomore when he registered for my class in English 3 the following September. The record shows that all his grades at Texas were good except for an F in Physical Training—due no doubt to his refusal to recognize the existence of such a subject.

English 3 was an advanced course in composition wherein we studied Genung's *Rhetoric*, paid attention to grammar, and drilled on the architecture of sentences. The pupils read a good deal and wrote essays and narratives. They were not timid in criticizing each other's papers. This class of fourteen was the most distinguished in quality of individuals that I directed in my whole academic career. There was Anita Brenner, whose *Idols Behind Altars* and other books interpreting Mexico hold up well. The most mature mind in the class, not excluding the instructor's, was that of Prussian-born Hartman Dignowity, who knew Goethe, Darwin, Nietzsche, Wagner, and Shakespeare but needed to perfect his use of the English language. He considered Branch an amusing infant with perhaps more pretensions than powers. Another member of the class, Leeper Gay, introduced me to a character named Wes Burton across the river—the Colorado River—who had dedicated his life to hunting the Lost San Saba Mine. He and his parents and sister were storybook characters and led me a long way into what became the book entitled *Coronado's Children*.

I was at the time probably experimenting more in the craft of writing than any of my pupils. After being in the Field Artillery in World War I for about two years, I had come back to the University of Texas as an instructor, taught for a year, resigned to manage a big ranch down in the Brush Country, and now was back again among the academicians. My pupils were fresh human beings to me; Branch remains in my memory as the nearest to a genius I ever had.

He was delicate in body and limb, maybe not over five feet two or three inches tall, hardly weighing over 130 pounds. His complexion was of a virginal rose; he did not yet need to shave and had no down. He kept his black hair brushed down. His eyes, somewhat protruding, were extraordinarily bright and flashed when he was interested—and he habitually was. The talk was that he burned sandalwood in his room in order to inhale the fragrance. He would have burned mesquite or anything else in order to enjoy the reputation of being a character. I had read with avidity *Confessions of an Opium Eater* and saw in Branch a veritable simulacrum of De Quincey.

He had a disdain for pedestrian minds and announced himself a woman-hater. One of his class essays burned with contempt for perfumes used by young women to disguise other odors. To regard Branch's small figure and then to hear his bass voice was to be startled even after one knew him well. That voice was his passport to virility, though he was never garrulous and was quiet in conversation. He tended to reserve his booms for effect, just as he came to smoke a long, black cigar in public. Wilfred Scawen Blunt said of Nietzsche, promoter of the doctrine of Teutonic superiority, "He admires strength because he is physically a weakling. He despises women because he does not know them." I never had much affection for Branch, but he was interesting to me forty years ago and has been interesting to me ever since. Here I shall quote from reminiscences of Branch kindly written down for me by my friend Hartman Dignowity.

His knowledge of literature awed everyone in our class, including, I believe, Mr. Dobie. One day I found him in the library looking through catalogue cards and writing down titles of books by authors mentioned in an essay we were reading. He was not embarrassed to confide in me that should Mr. Dobie ask questions about these writers—as was his habit—he could by glibly rattling off titles of their works leave the impression that he was familiar with them. Dobie stopped me one day on the campus and commented on Branch's wide knowledge of past and contemporary literature. I did not give Branch away.

His physical appearance almost conditioned his attitudes. A pince nez secured by a black ribbon around his neck was such an obvious affectation that girls giggled when they saw him—but hardly ever gave him a second look. Walking through the state capitol one time, we were about to pass an old woman soliciting funds for crippled and sick children when she addressed her appeal to him. He adjusted his glasses, looked straight into her eyes and said: "I am adamant. Let the children die," and walked on. To me the play was most amusing. The old woman very likely did not know what *adamant* meant, but that word, look, and gesture left her gasping.

At Zerchausky's, a near-beer garden, once the Bismarck Saloon, he would order beer and rye bread with cheese or German sausage. I always felt that his drinking and eating there were affectation from a desire to appear masculine. He was not eager to pay for our repasts. His favorite author at this time was Ambrose Bierce.

One could not take the B.A. degree at the University of Texas without credit for mathematics or, as a substitute for mathematics, Greek. In the fall of 1923 Branch went to the State University of Iowa, where academic requirements were more to his liking. He received the A.B. degree in the spring of 1924 and the M.A. a year later. His chief mentor at Iowa was Dr. Louis Pelzer, professor of American history, who directed his thesis, "The Historical Foundations of the Fiction of the Ranch and Range." Pelzer showed a copy of the thesis to a representative of D. Appleton and Company, New York. In the fall of 1926 that publisher brought out *The Cowboy and His Interpreters*, by Douglas Branch. Branch gave me to understand that the book is substantially the thesis.

He did not want the public to know that the author was a twenty-one-year-old academician who had probably never been on a ranch and who would have been wretched had he been forced to live and work on one. He had asked me to write an introduction. I sent it. The publishers, he replied, said that it would "ruin him." He seemed relieved by their decision. They were advertising him as "born and raised in the heart of the cow country." Perhaps only cow people would know from what is not said as well as from what is said in the book that he had never associated with cows, followed a cow trail, or drunk water out of a cow track. The best of imaginations can flourish in authenticity only through a mastery of facts. What I said that "would ruin" the book was later put into a review, from which I quote: "Douglas Branch is not a cowboy, and is the first Texan to interpret cowboys without claiming to be one." While pointing out specific misrepresentations, I said much in favor of the book. It remains readable, and valid.

A college lad could not be expected to produce a mature book, but Branch was an intellectual and was already enjoying play of mind upon any subject that he treated. He did not know life and therefore could not be expected to know cowboys. He was moving toward a critical attitude. "There was no driving to do; the cattle moved of their own free will as in ordinary travel." Thus Branch quotes from Andy Adams' *The Log of a Cowboy*. Then he observes: "And the narrative itself seems to move of its own free will—leisurely, sure of itself, as natural as the trail men themselves. There are no grim, firm-lipped heroes among them, engrossed in their own humorless melodramas. Zane Grey would not know what to do with them." Branch is freer, and therefore better, interpreting the interpreters than the cowboys themselves. It is fine to prance when you are twenty, but pretense is something else. After all, as compared to the pretenses of piety and greed, the pretense of having sweated in a cowpen is very innocent.

During 1923–1925 I was head of the English Department at Oklahoma A.&M. College. In the summer of 1925 I gave Branch his first teaching job. To the descendants of Oklahoma squatters he was an oddity beyond their world, but for all I know they got along well enough together. He had a fellowship the following academic year at Ohio State University. He was working on the buffalo; also, to quote a letter of December 9, 1925, "reading such stuff as Strabo and Lucian, and smoking prodigiously." The following April he summed up his gainings in Columbus thus: "Material for the buffalo opus, four or five fine acquaintances, and bronchitis." Notice his precision in saying *acquaintances* rather than *friends*. He was hoping to get a job teaching history at the University of Texas or some other university to the west.

What he got was the professorship of American history at Louisiana Industrial Institute at Ruston—$3,000, 130 students, and "I am my own department." He was feeling his oats. To quote from a Louisiana letter: "I had a note from Andy Adams designating me as the chief of his many press agents." (This is an allusion to *The Cowboy and His Interpreters*.) "I thought that if the eminent Andy could afford to insert the word *many* I could afford not to answer the note." He had been to New York and in a Shubert revue seen "nudes that were not nudes but simply so much meat. . . ."

In 1927–1928 he was back at the State University of Iowa, where in June of 1928 he was granted the Ph.D.—the youngest recipient, it has been said, of the degree in that university's history. His thesis was on "The Utilization, Recession, and Near-Extermination of the American Bison." Under title of *The Hunting of the Buffalo* it was published by

Appleton in January, 1929. Branch had decided that his name would carry more weight if it had an initial prefixed to it; from then on his books were by E. Douglas Branch. Branch knew that he was writing a book and not a thesis. The buffalo book is more mature than *The Cowboy and His Interpreters*. Here scoffing has developed into irony. "I trust you," he wrote, "to keep to yourself in any review the circumstance that the book is my Ph.D. thesis (reannotated, but hardly changed otherwise)."

It was absurd for Branch to take Pawnee Bill— perhaps the most flushing foreflusher yet produced by Oklahoma—as a consultant on the buffalo. Not to recognize downright Charles Goodnight as a main preserver of the buffalo was an error. Branch was still short of twenty-four years of age when the book was published. It transmutes skeletons into vitalities. Here once more the buffalo bull paws into the earth, bellows his challenges, and before his countless followers fights in mighty pride for life and leadership; once more the great fur companies compete in trading knives and whiskey for pemmican and robes; once more the plains warriors make their great surrounds on foot, then run down cows and bulls on Spanish horses. I would say that no better introduction to Branch at his best can be found than his gusto over Captain Meriwether

Lewis' description of the cooking and eating of *boudin blanc*. Gusto, sympathy for the subject, is not a common virtue. Branch had it, and sophistication never killed it in his writings. He never wrote a dull page or a fulsome sentence.

The year *The Hunting of the Buffalo* was published, Branch was in residence at the State University of Iowa, living on a grant from the Social Science Research Council. He was trying to locate a good teaching job. In July 1928 he reported an advance of $1,800 by Appleton for a "popular but substantial" history of the West. He had office space with Pelzer and a free run of the library, where, as Professor Ross Livingston remembers,

he would often spend all night working. He was kindly receptive to suggestions any professor made about his work, or even his personal appearance. On one occasion I explained to him that being small, short, and frail, he should select clothing that would not accentuate those characteristics. I suggested blunt-pointed collars, large ties, coats with short lapels, hat creased flat. When I saw him at a professional meeting in Des Moines sometime later, he had adopted some of my suggestions and good-humoredly asked me to look him over.

Like all of us, Branch responded kindly to kindness and was more humble-minded than many gave him credit for being. "You may be amazed to hear it," he said out loud in a letter of 1929, "but I have some modesty, and I don't expect to write—or be able to write—a first-rate book for half a dozen years yet."

At the same time he could say, "I'm profoundly convinced of the truth of my own prejudices only in matters of literary principles. I hate Dreiser, Suckow, and Harriet Monroe with a beautiful and holy hate —with James Joyce and Zane Grey in the tier just below them." After a final examination in contemporary American fiction at Iowa, as his instructor John T. Frederic recollects, Branch "expressed his opinion of one of the books assigned (Ruth Suckow's *Country People*) by tearing his copy to bits and depositing them in a wastebasket up front—to the excitement of the class." He was never, understand, a book-burner—but Cyrano de Bergerac was one of his admirations. "What a gesture!"

A career as historian of the West "may not be what I would have chosen; it may not be the thing I'm best suited for. But I shall tackle this history of the West honestly and with a little humility." Thus Branch viewed himself soon after accepting $1,800 to carry out some hack editor's idea of a book. Before it got published—and neglected—he was (May 16, 1929) proposing a life of Ramsay Crooks of the American Fur Company. What became of that project is unknown to me.

Westward, an economically written book of around 200,000 words, running to 627 pages, counting the index, appeared in 1930. The Great Depression had struck, and Branch never recovered from the blow. About a year following publication of *Westward*, he wrote me: "When I survey that unwieldy edifice I feel three kinds of a fool. The fact that I was sick as a pup summer before last is no excuse for my having dodged the simple drudgery of verification that would have made it nearly a first-rate book. I wonder if anybody ever learns anything." The book is better than Branch rated it, though not well proportioned. It starts in with "when Massachusetts was West," but hardly gets to the end of the nineteenth century. Here, as elsewhere, Branch is particular, concrete, selective of detail; I used to quote Blake to the class he was in: "To generalize is to be an idiot. Knowledge consists of particulars." To me, the first part of *Westward* is fresher, more vivid than the latter, which takes in the Wild West.

A new field for Branch was women. Early in 1929

he wrote, rather simperingly I thought, of a young lady in Washington who had made an impression upon his heart. She was not the Perla whom he married and with whom he was living in New York in 1931, hard up for money and a job. According to one of his friends, she was "capable"; according to another, bride and groom were both attractive. "He was extremely well groomed, sharp featured, and had clear, keen eyes back of modest, rimless spectacles. His wife was nothing short of beautiful. She was properly demure, as the wife of a successful, rising young author, with an oral mastery of historical wisdom and a genius at phrase making, should be. All in all, our evening visit with the couple was very pleasant, but it was apparent that a sharp tongue and oracular opinionation were his worst enemies."

In March of 1932 Branch's mother wrote me from Houston asking that I try to find a job for Douglas. I had tried; there were no jobs. She said that he was "beginning to assume an inferiority complex" and that his parents were educating another son and could hardly spare money to Douglas. In a jaunty letter received from him a few days earlier he spoke in an offhand way of reviewing books for "Cole." My expressing ignorance of the editor brought this retort:

The "Cole" whose name I used with a familiarity you found arrant is simply the editor of the *Mississippi Valley Historical Review*, which quarterly I humbly assumed you read once in a while. As for the editors of publications that pay money to their authors, I am sorrowful (as a homeless author) and proud (as a gentleman) that I don't know any. I have met quite a few, but that's something else again.

If Perla and I can, by some sheer miracle of the "dismal science," provide ourselves with bed and board, I shall have completed, by the first of June, my masterpiece; my relict can pay for her weeds with the royalties. The book will begin with the Great Fire of December 16, 1835, in New York City and conclude at about the time Mr. George B. Jocelyn, railroad agent of Vincennes, Indiana, wrote the three social degrees (Love, Equality, and Fraternity) of the Knights Templars. Since I cannot find a market, I had as well do what I want to do, and write a good book.

The "good book" Branch was to complete by the first of June did not get published until 1934. By then Perla had divorced him and become a detective exercising surveillance over employees for a chain of stores. Meanwhile Branch's publishers had through a merger become D. Appleton-Century Company. The title of the book is *The Sentimental Years: 1836-1860*.

As *Westward* is a social history with emphasis on place and time, *The Sentimental Years* is a social history with emphasis on people—their manners, hypocrisies, greeds, credulities, also sincerities and other attributes. Rich in irony, wit, and urbanity, vivid in Macaulay-like details, deft in craftsmanship, it is Branch's ripest work. Here he is sophisticated where sophistication fits. Compassion has come to him; patronization has gone away.

"The machinery of government was intrusted to a convenient element, the professional politicians— who maintained themselves by being professional democrats." John Bartholomew Gough, firebrand of the Temperance Movement, "offered a creed of self-perfectibility by perfecting the conduct of other people." Textile laborers in Massachusetts worked eleven hours a day. In an election year "the Hamilton Company had a notice posted on the factory gate: 'Whoever, employed by this corporation, votes the Ben Butler Ten-Hour ticket will be discharged.'" In the South, Scott's *Ivanhoe* "coddled the illusion of a second age of chivalry."

Probably the most congenial position of Branch's life was as associate professor of English and history at Montana State University (called also University of Montana) at Missoula. Here he found a friend in Professor Harold Merriam, with whom he enjoyed editing *Frontier and Midland*. "An excellent gentleman," he characterized Merriam to me, "but a frustrated idealist, hence of unpredictable whim." It was hard for him to resist a lance. I don't know if he ever loved anybody; he truly liked his friend and mentor Dr. Louis Pelzer and realized a debt to him, but this remark was passed around as a Branch cut: "I wrote my thesis under a wooden-minded professor who didn't know a social significance from a whirlwind."

In September, 1936, "on a postman's holiday in Missoula," he wrote: "I lost something of human peace and quite a little divinity under my feet by leaving Montana [in the fall of 1935] for a full professorship and a meet wage at the Cathedral of Learning" (the University of Pittsburgh in a skyscraper). While in Pittsburgh he was for a time paid secretary of the Historical Society of Western Pennsylvania. His published books—four in nine years— were all behind him. At twenty-nine his writing career was over.

On August 10, 1939, he sent out the following announcement from Pittsburgh, Pennsylvania:

On Friday, July 28, 1939 at Winchester, Virginia, Dr. E. Douglas Branch and one

Helen Schmidt, an excellent and comely person, were united to mutual gratulations.

The immediately present family comprises one Kitten which sleeps with us, and three Turtles which do not.

Dr. Branch regrets that a broken right hand precludes his scribbling, for a few weeks, the personal amenities which accompany this message.

That hand gave him increasing trouble. The "excellent and comely person" was a grass widow with a child. On July 4, 1942—and it had been a long time between letters—he wrote me from Chicago: "I left the gilded hypocrisy of Pittsburgh almost coincidentally with our entrance into the war. Am 4-F myself, thanks to two (the maximal quota per person, I believe) broken hands: no actual handicap, save that I cannot lift and carry anything. I've been working on a couple of 'patriotic' programs at CBS here. . . .

"I have become a Number One aillurophile [defined in the next letter as cat-lover], specializing in confused breeds; we have three beautiful bastards now." That *we* would indicate that the "excellent and comely person" with whom he and "one Kitten" were sleeping in 1939 was still the wife of Dr. E. Douglas Branch. She did not so remain much longer. About this time he went west again for a year with Montana State College at Bozeman.

By now he had become, among historians of the Mid-West, a kind of legend for brilliance—soon to be a brilliance impaired by drink in the Edgar Allan Poe pattern. His presence at any meeting of the Mississippi Valley Historical Association was marked. "At midnight the year the M.V.H.A. met at Vincennes," to quote Walker D. Wyman of Wisconsin State College, "Branch had not yet written a paper to be delivered the following day. By ten the next morning it was down on paper—in publishable form."

In the fall of 1945 he got a part-time teaching job with Roosevelt University, supplemented by one with the Chicago Undergraduate Division of the University of Illinois. His work at Roosevelt warranted his being given a special course in the spring term. Within two months he was missing so many classes or showing up in such a state of incoherent drunkenness that there was "no alternative to releasing him." Off and on during the forties he ground out articles for the *American Peoples Encyclopedia* in Chicago under the editorship of Franklin J. Meine, writing "a large part of American history material in the early volumes." Too much alcoholism lost him this connection, but his work—astonishingly rapid—was so excellent that the *Encyclopedia* put up with him even after he was no longer dependable.

For part of the academic year 1946–1947 his flickering candle made a—locally—fine light at Center College, Danville, Kentucky. The following is from a recorded interview with John Hakac, presently with the University of Arizona.

That year I was taking Freshman English under a couple of jackasses at Center. Dr. Branch had the maturest and brightest students in a Shakespeare course. He was a celebrated campus character. Danville was dry, but Lexington, forty miles away, wasn't. A bus that left Lexington about 2 A.M. on Sunday mornings was usually loaded with more or less drunken students. Frequently Dr. Branch would climb and stumble aboard among them, always carrying a leather satchel making *clink, clink, clink* sounds. Some student would say, "What do you have there, Dr. Branch?" He would reply, "Records," and ride back to Danville in a stupor.

He wore army clothes, GI olive drabs, even a

khaki tie. Some students declared that he went a month without changing his clothes; dress in no way dented his appeal. They loved him, sympathized with him. When we heard that Dr. Branch was the author of books, we undergraduates ran to the library to gaze upon a book by a man who walked among us in the flesh. One student declared *The Hunting of the Buffalo* good reading but objectionable on account of the punctuation. He had counted twenty-six semicolons, he said, on one page. They interrupted his interest. Periods would have been all right. Faulkner, without any punctuation at all, would have been better.

Dr. Branch was living alone in one room. According to student belief, his wife had died in a fire and his resultant suffering was so great that he took to the bottle and lived in utter loneliness. The end of the semester (1947) came and Branch had not turned in his final grades. The deadline passed and still no grades were in. I'm just telling what was common talk. The college dean went to Branch's room and knocked on the door. He got no answer, walked in anyhow, and found Dr. Branch drunk in bed. Rousing him slightly, he asked if the final grades were ready. Dr. Branch said no. "Get up and get these grades. We need them," the dean admonished. Branch remained supine. The dean now suggested that he would read the class roll and Branch could say off A, B, C, D, etc., as an estimated grade. Branch agreed. Most of the class were GI's. Finally the dean came to a Mr. Smith. "I can't recall that name at all," Branch said. The dean identified Mr. Smith in some way. "Oh, yes," Branch cried, "I remember him now. Give him an A—poor devil, he's married."

Back in Chicago, to which he always returned, Branch tried to get a counter job with the Thompson restaurant chain but failed to pass the required physical examination. During this period he got a job in some West Virginia college, but it didn't last. Occasionally he reviewed a book for the Chicago *Sun*. He no longer associated with his peers and they no longer loaned him small sums. His shirts and suits became seedier, his skin more flushed, his hands more tremulous, his nervous sweat more profuse, his deep voice out of such a small and wasted body more haunting. Professor Kendall B. Taft, of Roosevelt University, solicited and obtained aid for him from writing men over the nation. Branch had cut his hand on a bread-slicer. From now on there would for him be no respite from Skid Row, sometimes washing dishes in cheap eating places, sometimes serving at the counter, sometimes waiting on tables, sometimes just sitting. In response to one letter written during his long, long downhill stumbling I sent money to buy a cheap suit of clothes. Something soon happened to the suit—if the few dollars went for it. The following letter tells all one needs to know about Grub Street existence in one American city by one ruined writer.

DEAR J. FRANK:

I am in most rarefiedly refreshed mood, just having read Eudora Welty's *The Robber Bridegroom* for the first time, and raptly.

I began the New Year auspiciously by picking up a banner [translation: responding to a "Waiter Wanted" sign in the window] at 1 A.M., January the first, and I surmise I may do as well at 10 tonight, since I have seen a waiter due to take up his shift there who has taken up too much already.

Thank goodness I am nimble, if I have no strength. There is so little I can do, of the work arrantly (and mistakenly) called "unskilled." What chance I had for a college appointment last fall was effectivey wrecked by the collusion of the College Specialists Bureau and the Chicago post-office.

I have so much to write, and see so little likelihood that I shall. But this is 1950; the thrice broken right hand may almost be called dextrous again, and the sinister hand has acquired dexterity.

My rent and my larder run four days ahead at the moment, which is good. One week in October, after a hebdomad of inanition to give my coccyx opportunity to half-forget my annual Slip on the Ice, I spent three nights of five as a non-ordering table-sitter in various restaurants where I am known; and I have learned that the only thing really to dread is to be utterly out of tobacco.

The smug Babbitts who think of "clerical positions" and the like have no realization that bed and food are not salvered instanter on the first day, that swans do not furnish one with eider nor ravens with matzoth, to bridge the appalling gap until the first check. Random catering, with the hope of a culinary liaison of duration (and how little turnover there is now! How rabid and hungry the competition!)—the horizon goes little farther. Sans contact; sans lectern or swivel.

But there are worse. And I read until I know it an opiate.

The very best of 1950 for you

DOUGLAS

On July 18, 1954, I was in Missoula, Montana. The *Daily Missoulian* of that morning printed an

Associated Press dispatch from Helena saying that Dr. E. Douglas Branch, former instructor at Montana State University and Montana State College, had died in Chicago July 10, three days after his forty-ninth birthday. Several years before this he had virtually disappeared from the world that once knew him.

I can offer no better conclusion than a paragraph in a letter from his friend Kendall B. Taft of Roosevelt University:

"His is a genuinely tragic fall of valor. To one who knew Douglas at his best, there could be no question about his brilliance, his wit, and his potential charm. He had a remarkable, though brief, period of productivity. Where the flaw lay, I do not know. His alcoholism was very probably a symptom, rather than a basic cause, of his moral deterioration. I do not judge him, God knows, but have only a profound regret that one so gifted should have been defeated—for whatever cause—by the demands of life."

Preface

A truthful narrative — this one is! — might well start with a whopping lie. The wild oat sowed before the tape jumps up, perhaps this book can run its course unrepressed, and finish still vigorous and still pure.

The whopper is from a tale in Hakluyt's *Voyages* (I like people who read Hakluyt, and I have written in the faith that some of them will like this narrative of the buffalo), a relation of the strange experiences and adventures of Friar Marcos de Niza, who visited the Pueblo Indians in 1539. At one of his stopping-places, says the Friar, "they shewed me an hide halfe as bigge againe as the hide of a great oxe, and told me that it was the skin of a beaste, which had but one horne upon his forehead, and that this horne bendeth toward his breast, and that out of the same goeth a point right forward, wherein he hath so great strength, that it will breake any thing how strong so ever it be, if he runne against it, and that there are great store of these beastes in that country."

The myth of the unicorn, however, is only a little more monstrous than the fact of the buffalo.

There must once have been thirty million buffaloes roaming a vast range of American prairies and forests; when Grover Cleveland was moving into the White House a second time, there were about a thousand and ninety, and nearly all of these were in far northern fastnesses or in captivity. The thirty million had been hunted down — hunted, shot, pierced, impounded, tricked, for the fun of it, for the money in it, for the necessity of it. It was an awful, epic hunt—a story that demands to be told honestly and dispassionately, or not at all.

The range of the buffalo included the Mississippi delta, the Pennsylvania mountains, northern Mexico, the upper shores of Great Slave Lake; it enveloped nearly two-fifths of the entire area of North America. The restriction of this range, gradual, then suddenly ruthless; the coming of new peoples who hunted; the ways, the tools, the laws of the hunt: that is the meat of this narrative. Naturally, emphasis is given that loud, lusty frontier of the eighteen-seventies and eighteen-eighties, when the western herd of over seven million buffaloes was shattered and annihilated, and barely eighty scarred fugitives were left. This buffalo hunters' frontier sprang up with so little warning, and collapsed with such inglorious speed, that it has missed its share of attention; the history of the buffalo hunt is almost as scattered as the buffalo bones left to moulder on the prairies. I have tried to do a decent job of picking up the pieces.

Dedication is a rather ineffective way of repaying courtesies; but that method has the sanction of custom. I gladly recognize the claims of several men to this little flourish: Major Gordon W. Lillie ("Pawnee Bill"), who has given me the benefit of his ancient and honorable acquaintance with the buffalo; Tom Branch, gentleman and Texan; Louis Pelzer, the chronicler of the cattle trade, and J. Frank Dobie, the Texas folk-lorist, whose encouraging halloos have been as gustable to me as broiled buffalo marrow. But precedence seems to belong to that huge, handsome buffalo bull who stood for so many years in the foyer of the town auditorium in Houston, Texas. Crowds used to pass by him of an evening, to hear Mr. Taft upon the freedom of judges, to see "Chu Chin Chow," to witness Plestina sweating to get a toehold on the Wrestling Trust; whatever the occasion, he stared through them and past them all, through even the matty black frontlet that overhung his glassy eyes. There was a faint touch of regal contempt in that immobile stare; there was, it seemed to the youngster who saw him often, the self-pride that distinguishes a good loser.

E. D. B.

State Historical Society of Iowa,
Iowa City

CONTENTS

CONTENTS

Illustrations

The Hunting of the Buffalo

CHAPTER I

THE PERSONS IN THE DRAMA

THE Apache tribe had no food except the seeds of two plants, when a sharp-eyed Indian discovered that the raven ate meat. The tribe followed the raven, at a discreet distance, and came to a great circle of ashes where the ravens were accustomed to cook their meals. There was no getting at the secret without magic. So a medicine man transformed a boy into a puppy; the ravens found him and adopted him. At sunset the puppy peeped from his covers, and saw an old raven brush aside the ashes of the fireplace, and remove a large stone which disclosed an opening into the underworld; through the opening he disappeared, and came back shortly with a buffalo, which the ravens killed and ate. For four sunsets the little puppy watched this descent; but on the fifth day he changed himself back into a boy, and went into the opening. When he emerged he brought with him all the animals at present upon the surface of the earth. They were led by the buffalo, the king of the animals.

Somewhere in the lore of nearly all the Indian tribes whom American explorers found on the Great Plains is an echo of the first sharp surprise when the tribe found the buffalo.[1] And whatever might be the tribe's own culture myth, of how some young man of great magic first brought the buffalo droves to his starving people, or how the tribe's animal deity taught the braves to hunt, the tradition crystallized among the Plains Indians that the buffalo were produced in countless numbers in a country under the ground; that every spring they swarmed out of great cavelike exits, somewhere in the Staked Plains of northwest Texas. Tribes on the Canadian plain placed the exit to the buffaloes' underworld somewhere southwest of the Eagle Hills, in a lake whose waters never rested: "See, it is from under that lake that our buffalo comes. You say they are all gone; but look, they come again and again to us. We cannot kill them all—they are there under that lake. Do you hear the noise which never ceases? It is the buffalo fighting with each other far down under the ground, and striving to

[1] For buffalo lore in Amerind folk tales, see E. Douglas Branch, "Buffalo Lore and Boudin Blanc," *Publications of the Texas Folk-Lore Society,* V, and the volumes by G. B. Grinnell, G. A. Dorsey, and Frances Densmore, there cited. Fascinating tales are scattered through the *Journal of American Folk-Lore;* see volume indices.

get out upon the prairie—where else can they come from?"

The buffalo moved and grazed in herds; they were migratory animals. These are two laws of the behavior of the buffalo which may be taken for granted. But between Catlin's denial that the herds actually migrated, and the beautiful statement of the Abbé Emmanuel Domenech: "Buffaloes are of a timorous nature, and willingly seek the neighborhood of men," lie many attempts to endow the buffalo with social intelligence, to give the buffalo bull a sense of his responsibilities as a father and a polygamist. There were just as many frontiersmen, however, who would swear that a buffalo cow always led the herd as there were those who were sure that a big, vigorous bull was always the leader. A single herd of buffalo might actually number twenty, or two hundred; and often many small herds were assimilated into one herd of ten thousand buffalo or ten million.[2]

Nor were the migrations to be determined surely. The great waves of migration swept southward with

[2] Among the standard natural histories, those of E. T. Seton and of Audubon and Bachmann offer good descriptions of the buffalo and the buffalo's habits; best is the account in W. T. Hornaday, "The Extermination of the American Bison," *Smithsonian Institution: Report of the United States National Museum*, 1887. Occasionally in the course of this narrative I have rested squarely upon Hornaday's labor.

J. A. Allen's long-scarce monograph, "The American Bison Living the approach of winter, and northward with the thaw; but buffaloes that spent the summer near the upper Saskatchewan went in the seasonal migration to the plains below Lake Winnipeg, more nearly east than south. A seasonal migration was from about two hundred and fifty miles to four hundred and fifty miles in length. As long as the buffalo could roam at will, there was no great surge of all the millions of these animals in the West in a body, from the limits of the summer range to the southern range; but there were three, perhaps four, regional divisions of migration—so that, for instance, the herds that grazed in summer on the Grand Coteau des Prairies of the Saskatchewan traveled with the coming of winter into Montana, and the buffalo that had summered on the ranges of Montana and North Dakota made a winter migration into Nebraska, Wyoming, and northern Colorado.

The southern migration was the more desultory, the less organized, of the two annual journeys. After rainy summers, when the grass had escaped parching, the migration was slow and delayed. It is the northward migration which awed the travelers in the buffalo range. Colonel Richard Irving Dodge, stationed on the Arkansas River from 1869 to 1873,

and Extinct,'' *Memoirs of the Geological Survey of Kentucky,* Vol. I, and simultaneously (1875) in *Memoirs of the Museum of Comparative Zoölogy, at Harvard College,* Vol. IV, is still unsuperseded in its work of tracing the geographical limits of the bison herds.

had opportunity to study this migration: "Early in spring, as soon as the dry and apparently desert prairie had begun to change its coat of dingy brown to one of palest green, the horizon would begin to be dotted with buffalo, single, or in groups of two and three, forerunners of the coming herd. Thicker and thicker, and in larger groups they come, until by the time the grass is well up, the whole vast landscape appears a mass of buffalo, some individuals feeding, others lying down, but the herd moving slowly, moving constantly to the northward. . . . Some years, as in 1871, the buffalo appeared to move northward in one immense column, oftentimes from twenty to fifty miles in width, and of unknown depth from front to rear. Other years the northward journey was made in several parallel columns, moving at the same rate and with their numerous flankers covering a width of a hundred or more miles."

Unlike domestic cattle, the buffalo ran against the wind, and in a winter storm stood facing the wind. In fierce snowstorms, when the hunter had to dig himself a hole in the snow and remain wrapped in his blankets until the storm passed, the threatened buffaloes huddled together in compact masses, those on the outside crowding and fighting to get to the inside, and the herd kept warm by the jostling. The buffalo were very often in poor condition by the end of winter; but only in very exceptional years were many of them killed by winter rigors. In the far northern area between Peace River and Hay River, a snowstorm of 1820, or about that year, deposited fourteen feet of snow in a few days, and the enveloped buffalo perished by tens of thousands.

Thousands of buffalo were drowned each spring, when the thawing ice of streams and lakes crackled under the rush of the migrating herd. The upper waters of the Missouri were each year clogged with drowned buffaloes. One of the small rivers emptying into the Republican is called (to the grief of the Wyoming legislature) the Stinking Water, a name conferred by Indians, who had several times been forced to abandon a camp site on this stream because of the numbers of buffalo that had been fast mired in the mud. John McDonnell, descending the Qu'Appelle River in the spring of 1795, put in a whole May day in counting the drowned and mired buffaloes; when his party camped for the evening he had counted seven thousand, three hundred and sixty. "It is true, in one or two places I went on shore and walked from one carcass to the other, where they lay from three to five files deep."

The rutting season of the buffalo was from early July to late September. Grazing on the nutritious grama grass, every buffalo in the herd had grown sleek and vigorous. The small herds had come together in one great, dense mass; and in the confusion of roaring and running, bellowing and tramping, the volume of noise rolled, said plainsmen, two or three miles away. John Bradbury, the English naturalist, found the herd in rutting season: "The males were fighting in every direction, with a fury which I have never seen paralleled, each having singled out his antagonist. There were many hundreds of these battles going on at the same time, some not eighty yards from us. A shot was fired amongst them, which they seemed not to notice." Thanks to the thickness of the hide and pelage on the head and shoulders of the bulls, these battles preliminary to choosing mates were nearly always harmless. At the close of the rutting season the great herd gradually resolved itself into little foraging bands again.

The calving season was in late spring. It was the habit of the cows to leave the bulls at calving time; but as soon as the invigorating sun allowed the calves to take a place in the herd, the bulls assumed the duty of protecting them from the wolves that haunted the rim of the herd. An army surgeon told Colonel Dodge of seeing "a little knot of six or eight buffalo, all bulls, standing in a close circle with their heads outwards, while in a concentric circle at some twelve or fifteen paces distant sat, licking their chops in impatient expectancy, at least a dozen large grey wolves. . . . After a few minutes the knot broke up, and, still keeping in a compact mass, started on a trot for the main herd, some half a mile off. The central and controlling figure of this mass was a poor little calf, so newly born as scarcely to be able to walk. After going fifty or a hundred paces the calf lay down, the bulls disposed themselves in a circle as before, and the wolves, who had trotted along on each side of their retreating supper, sat down again. . . ." Once a buffalo calf, pursued by a pack of wolves, broke through General Fremont's camp. One buffalo bull was near, and attacked the wolves, but the pack was too many; and the calf was half devoured before he was dead.

The buffalo bull was the grandest ruminant in nature; and in the grand setting of the trans-Mississippi West his majesty was the unvarying comment of travelers. His weight reached two thousand pounds; his height at his hump was six feet, and perhaps two or three inches more; in length he was over ten feet. The massive, magnificent head never lost its thick frontlet and its beard. The winter pelage of the body was a rich fur, of a color Audubon called "between a dark umber and liver-shining brown."

And when this spectacular beast was tired of providing a tableau, he could create his own drama.

On an afternoon in early summer, a few lazy men were in a clump of trees at the bank of the Missouri. Through a gap in the grove they saw a mass of dark-brown shoulders slowly moving toward the river. They could hear the rasping sound as the buffalo crunched the grama grass. They caught another sound: the van of another herd was surmounting a hill.

Each herd discovered the other at about the same time, and came to a standstill for a moment; then the buffalo of each herd began again to crunch the grass in a slow march forward. The space separating the herds was slowly reduced; and the two leading bulls approached each other like two freight engines determined to run head-on.

The bull whose herd had been first on the prairie announced his rage, pawing the earth, and with his horns tossing up bunches of sod that silted down into his mane. The later arrival likewise curved up flumes of dirt with his hooves, and tore into the earth with his horns. The two bulls came nearer, and the herds left off their crunching to watch.

After much circling and side-stepping for position, the fighters made the rush—with a heavy collision of skulls and a crash of horns. Then they pushed, head against head; muscles bulged out on thighs, and hooves wrenched into the earth. They pushed, until one of them went down on his knees.

That settled it. The conquering bull scraped his horns into the hide and flesh of his victim; and he left off the taunts to meander into his adversary's herd. But as he strode, another bull moved his monstrous bulk out of the herd, and snorted another challenge.

The contestants squared off, and plunged. The thud of the collision threw them both to their knees; but both were instantly on their feet, and locked horns with the same swiftness.

"The cords stood out like great ropes on their necks; the muscles on thighs and hips were like huge welts. We were quite near these fellows and could see the roll of their blood-red fiery eyes. They braced and shoved with perfectly terrible force. The froth began to drip in long strings from their mouths."

The erstwhile victor slipped slightly from one foothold; his antagonist swung forward, but the champion tightened his back-muscles, and forced the challenger to a standstill.

Both relaxed a moment for breath, then sank their hooves into the sod and renewed the struggle. A sound came like the crack of lightning as one of the legs of the champion crumpled under him. The challenger lunged toward him, to finish the fight; then the earth trembled, the fighters reeled, and the bluff on which the two buffaloes were standing dropped into the Missouri, and the current bore the actors downstream.[3]

And after twenty-five years of vigorous life—the wolves, or the coyotes. The old bulls, gaunt and stiff from age and spotted and torn with scars, were prey to the packs that skulked at the herd's edge. Coyotes did not dare attack an old, isolated patriarch; as long as the bull kept his feet, he lived. But a system of worrying him, of giving him no rest, would win; and as he tottered from exhaustion, his enemies leaped, bit, and held.

.   .   .   .   .   .

The story that white men know of the American buffalo begins with the end of a civilization: when Montezuma Xocoyotzin, ninth king of Mexico, was found with chains about his feet and five dagger wounds in his breast, and the legionaries of Hernando Cortes soon laid the Aztec Empire with its king.

Within his capital the emperor had maintained, for the instruction of his people, a menagerie: "In the second Square of the same House were the Wild Beasts, which were either presents to Montezuma, or taken by his Hunters, in strong Cages of Timber, rang'd in good Order, and under cover: Lions, Tygers, Bears, and all others of the savage kind

[3] Alexander Majors, *Seventy Years on the Frontier* (Chicago and New York, 1893).

[11]

which New-Spain produced; among which the greatest Rarity was the Mexican Bull, a wonderful composition of divers Animals. It has crooked shoulders, with a Bunch on its back like a Camel; its Flanks dry, its Tail large, and its Neck covered with Hair like a Lion. It is cloven footed, its Head armed like that of a Bull, which it resembles in Fierceness, with no less Strength and Agility."

This "wonderful composition" was the first buffalo seen by Europeans. More than twenty years passed before Europeans saw the buffalo uncaged and in its natural home.

When the Spanish people were attempting to thrust the Moors from the Peninsula into the Mediterranean, a poor shepherd had pointed the way of the army to victory, marking the mountain path the Spaniards should choose with the skull of a cow.[4] The King of Navarre gave the shepherd the name of Cabeza de Vaca. A descendant, Alvar Nunez Cabeza de Vaca (skull-of-a-cow), led the first expedition of white men into the "wild cow" country.

It was a bedraggled remnant of a pompous expedition that first saw the buffalo, on the plains of Texas. A force of 600 colonists and soldiers, bearing a grant from His Most Catholic Majesty to conquer and possess all the country between Florida and

[4] The battle of Las Navas de Tolosa, July, 1212.

eastern Mexico, had been reduced, in 1633, to eight —and these eight dependent on the charity of a miserable, mosquito-plagued tribe of Indians, whose sustenance included lizards, snakes' eggs, and spiders. In writing of his stay among these Indians Cabeza de Vaca made note of the buffalo: "Cattle come as far as here. Three times have I seen them and eaten of their meat. . . . To my judgement the flesh is finer and fatter than that of this country (Spain). Of the skins of those not full grown the Indians make blankets, and of the larger they make shoes and bucklers. They come as far as the sea-coast of Florida, from a northerly direction, ranging through a tract of more than four hundred leagues; and throughout the whole region over which they run, the people who inhabit near, descend and live upon them, distributing a great many hides into the interior country." [5]

Three years later Cabeza de Vaca and three surviving companions appeared in the little Spanish settlement of Culiacán, near the Gulf of California. They had crossed North America from shore to shore. Their adventures awakened an appetite for knowledge, and prompted the expedition captained

[5] The records of these early explorations of the Southwest are easily accessible, in *Spanish Explorers in the Southern United States, 1528-1543*, ed. by F. W. Hodge and T. H. Lewis (New York, 1907), and *Spanish Exploration in the Southwest, 1542-1706*, ed. by, H. E. Bolton (New York, 1916).

by Francisco Vásquez Coronado ("There were so many men of high quality among the Spaniards, that such a noble body was never collected in the Indies, nor so many men of quality in such a small body, there being three hundred men") that was to bring the Spaniards some realization of the numbers and importance of these shaggy-haired, humped, terrifying "wild cows."

Before the army had reached the Seven Cities, the treasure-laden Cibola "somewhere in the north-west" that Coronado had hoped to rob, they were disillusioned. They knew that great cities were not to be found, nor any wealth of gold; and a private soldier, Pedro de Castenada, the chronicler of the expedition, put aside his ambitions and turned his interest to the scenes of their march. Of the wild life of this unknown north he first noticed the Rocky Mountain sheep, in the ranges of southeastern Arizona: "I myself saw and followed them. They had extremely large bodies and long wool; their horns were very thick and large, and when they run they throw back their heads and put their horns on the ridge of their back. They are used to the rough country, so that we could not catch them and had to leave them."

While they were at Cibola some Indians arrived from a village far to the east; they came, they said, to offer themselves as friends and guides. They

y enojan : finalmente es animal feo y fiero de ro-
ftro, y cuerpo. Huyé de los los cauallos por fu ma-
la catadura, o por nunca los auer visto. No tienen
fus dueños otra riqueza, ni hazienda, dellos co-
men, beuen, visten, calçan, y hazen muchas cosas
de los cueros, casas, calçado, vestido y sogas : delos
huessos, punçones : delos neruios, y pelos, hilo : de
los cuernos, buches, y bexigas, vasos : delas boñi-
gas, lumbre : y delas terneras, odres, en que traen
y tienen agua : hazen en fin tantas cosas dellos
quantas han menester, o quantas las bastan para
su biuienda. Ay tambien otros animales, tan grandes como cauallos, que por tener cuernos, y lana
fina, los llaman carneros, y dizen, que cada cuer-
no pesa dos arrouas. Ay tambien grandes perros,
que

OLDEST KNOWN PICTURE OF THE AMERICAN BISON
From Thevet's *Les Singularitez de la France Anarctique*
(Antwerp, 1558).

brought presents of tanned hides and shields and headpieces, all made from the buffalo; and Coronado gave them some glass dishes, some beads, and little bells—"which they prized highly, because these were things they had never seen." They described the great cows of their country; but Castenada doubted that they were cows, because the hides were covered with hair woolly and snarled, like nothing he had seen in Spain. The general ordered Hernando de Alvarado to take twenty companions and go with these Indians, to return after eighty days and give an account of what he had found.

These Indians brought the Spanish company into their village of Cicuye, in the Pecos valley. Alvarado struck up a friendship with an Indian slave here, a native of the region toward Florida. This Indian—called "Turk" by the Spaniards—had well learned the fancies that beguiled De Soto into the inland wilderness and to his destruction; and when Alvarado took him to guide the party to the "cows," he talked of an El Dorado rich in gold and silver. Alvarado no longer cared about looking for "cows," and turned back to join Coronado. The expedition listened to the "Turk," thereby losing the confidence of the western Indians; and again Spaniards set out after a mirage of wealth for the taking. But had it not been for the buffalo they killed and ate, this expedition would have starved.

Coronado's army entered the Texas Panhandle, into the country of the Apaches Vaqueros and farther westward into the hunting grounds of the Tejas Indians. These tribes lived almost entirely on the buffalo. Castenada was awed by their cuisine: "They dry the flesh in the sun, cutting it thin like a leaf, and when dry they grind it like meal to keep it and make a sort of sea soup of it to eat. A handful thrown into a pot swells it so as to increase very much. They season it with fat, which they always try to secure when they kill a cow. They empty a large gut and fill it with blood, and carry this around the neck to drink when they are thirsty. When they open the belly of a cow, they squeeze out the chewed grass and drink the juice that remains behind, because they say that this contains the essence of the stomach. They cut the hide open at the back and pull off the joints, using a flint as large as a finger, tied in a little stick, with as much ease as if working with a good iron tool. They give it an edge with their own teeth."

There were a great number of white wolves, he noticed, prowling about the rim of the buffalo herds. There were deer about; and rabbits, very numerous and "so foolish that those on horseback killed them with their lances."

Several times they came upon great herds of buffalo. Once those of the advance guard fired into some bulls at the edge of a large herd. The buffalo, wounded or frightened, fled, trampling over one another, until they came to a ravine. Buffaloes stumbled into the ravine until it was filled up, and the rest of the herd ran across over the backs of the heap in the ravine. Three horses, saddled and bridled, were swept into this stampede and lost.

When the expedition had returned, after two years of wandering that brought the Spaniards as far north as the north bank of the Kansas River, Castenada, gathering his impressions, dramatically described the buffalo: "It is to be noticed first that there was not one of the horses that did not take flight when he saw them first, for they have a narrow, short face, the brow two palms across from eye to eye, the eyes sticking out at the side, so that, when they are running, they can see who is following them. They have very long beards, like goats, and when they are running they throw their heads back with the beard dragging on the ground. There is a sort of girdle round the middle of the body. The hair is very long and rough like a camel's. They have a great hump, larger than a camel's. The horns are short and thick, so that they are not seen much above the hair. In May they change the hair in the middle of the body for a down, which makes perfect lions of them. They rub against the small trees in the ravines to shed their hair, and they continue this until only the down is left, like a snake changes his skin. They have a short tail, with a bunch of hair at the end. When they run they carry it erect like a scorpion." The buffalo plains were so level and smooth, he added, that if one looked at buffalo from a distance sky could be seen beneath their bodies, and the sight of one distant buffalo offered the illusion of four smooth-trunked pines whose tops joined.

The results of Coronado's expedition were disappointing; but forty years later eagerness for further exploration and for conquest of the Northwest was suddenly aroused, and in 1595 Juan de Onate, boasting the blood of both Cortes and Montezuma, received a grant of conquest and exploration, naming him captain general and governor.

From New Mexico in 1599 Onate wrote to the viceroy of the successes he had already won, and of his ambitions for Spain. He had, he reported, sent out his *sargento mayor,* Zaldivar, commanding a party of sixty, to "discover" the buffalo of the Great Plains to the northeast. Zaldivar's party had found the Indians very numerous in that country. They lived in tents of tanned buffalo hides, and moved their "rancherias" to follow the buffalo. "They eat meat almost raw, and much tallow and suet, which serves them as bread, and with a chunk of meat in one hand and a piece of tallow in the other, they bite first on one and then on the other, and grow up magnificently strong and courageous." They ambushed themselves in brush blinds near the watering places, and nearly always killed the buffalo with the first arrow.

Zaldivar attempted to capture some buffalo alive. Near the Canadian River, on a plain where the previous afternoon the party had seen "about a hundred thousand cattle," he had a corral constructed of cottonwood; but the buffaloes, instead of being tricked into the corral, directly stampeded the Spaniards. "It was impossible to stop them, because they are cattle so terribly obstinate, courageous beyond exaggeration, and so cunning that if pursued they run, and that if their pursuers stop or slacken their speed, they run and roll, just like mules, and with this respite renew their run." The buffalo killed three of the horses and tore gashes in forty. Recognizing that full-grown buffalo could not·be taken alive, Zaldivar ordered that calves be captured; "but they became so enraged that out of the many which were being brought, some dragged by ropes and others upon their horses, not one got a league toward the camp, for they all died within an hour." But the Spaniards did succeed in killing some buffalo, and found the meat of the buffalo cow greatly superior to any veal or mutton.

Zaldivar affected to be fascinated by the ugliness

of the buffalo: "Its shape and form are so marvelous and laughable, or frightful, that the more one sees it the more one desires to see it, and no one could be so melancholy that if he were to see it a hundred times a day he could keep from laughing heartily as many times, or could fail to marvel at the sight of so ferocious an animal. . . . In general, they are larger than our cattle. Their tail is like that of a hog, being very short, and having few bristles at the tip, and they twist it upward when they run. At the knees they have several garters of very long hair. In their haunches, which resemble those of mules, they are very hipped and crippled, and therefore run in leaps, especially down hill. They are all of the same color, somewhat tawny, in parts their hair being almost black. Such is their appearance, which at sight is far more ferocious than the pen can depict."

Onate visualized a thriving trade in the wool and the hides of the buffaloes. But the Spanish Empire was already a gouty, senile thing, sprawled over a vast area in sleepy inanition.

Franciscan monks found numerous herds of buffalo about Monterey; and there were buffaloes throughout northern Mexico. By the middle of the eighteenth century there were almost no buffalo north of the Rio Grande; but the upper waters of the Pecos, where Coronado had seen imposing herds, was always a winter home of the buffalo, and a last refuge when the animals were near extermination.

From Santa Fe and Taos, the northernmost settlements of the Spaniards in the Rio Grande country, wandering Mexicans set out to trade with the Indians; they brought a hard-tacklike bread, and sheet iron for arrow points, to exchange for the dressed buffalo skins and dried buffalo meat of the Indians. Cheyenne tradition says that these Mexicans went as far north as the Big Horn Mountains. The first expeditions of Americans to Santa Fe found solitary Mexican hunters, *ciboleros,* as far north as the dry bed of the Cimmaron.

In southern Texas the buffalo did not disappear until about 1825. Some bands apparently were not migratory, but fed all year on the perennial abundance of the banks of the Guadalupe and the Colorado.

Zebulon Montgomery Pike, describing Texas early in the nineteenth century, noted the abundance of wild animals—buffalo, deer, elk, and wild horses —and the influence of this plenty in turning the Spanish *emigrés* in Texas from the devout quiescence that their superiors desired of them: "Being on the frontiers where buffalo and wild horses abound in great numbers, and not engaged in any war with savages who are powerful, they have adopted a mode of living by following these animals, which has been productive of a more errant description round the capital (St. Antonio) than in any other of the provinces. But Cordero, by restricting (by edicts) the buffalo hunts to certain seasons, and obliging every man of family to cultivate so many acres of land, has in some degree checked the spirit of hunting, or wandering life, which had hitherto been so very prevalent; and has endeavored to introduce by example and precepts, a general urbanity and suavity of manners."

"Wild horses," Pike listed among the roaming animals of the Texas prairies. The first horses on the Texas plains were the mounts of Coronado's legionaries. In dribbles horses escaped, or were stolen, from their Spanish owners; they multiplied astonishingly, and droves of wild mustangs overspread the southern plains.

Indian tribes who had never seen a Spaniard profited by this sublime carelessness that let many horses escape the branding iron, and let many others be stolen by the southernmost tribes of Indians. Within the fifty years from 1675 to 1725 the life of the Plains Indian was reshaped by his acquisition of the horse. The ways of hunting buffalo were changed; and the game could be followed now in its migrations. Many cornfields and squash patches were not replanted. Tribes abandoned their earth

THE WILD DENIZENS OF THE PLAINS

From W. E. Webb, *Buffalo Land* (E. Hannaford, Chicago and Cincinnati, 1872).

lodges or wood lodges to live in light tepees of skin stretched on ridgepoles, houses that could be quickly dismounted or reassembled.

The Comanches and Apaches, living in the buffalo plains near the Spanish settlements in New Mexico and Texas, were the first tribes to use the horse; and it became so intimate a part of their lives that in 1850 the Comanches were boasting in all seriousness that the horse was created by the Good Spirit for the particular benefit of the Comanches, and that the Comanches had introduced it to the whites.

When American army expeditions penetrated into the Comanche country, they found these Indians the most expert in horsemanship of any of the western tribes. "He is in the saddle from boyhood to old age," Captain Marcy described the Comanche warrior, "and his horse is his constant companion. It is when mounted that the Comanche exhibits himself to the best advantage: here he is at home, and his skill at various maneuvers, such as throwing himself entirely upon one side of his horse, and discharging his arrows rapidly toward the opposite side from beneath the horse's neck while he is at full speed—is truly astonishing." Every warrior had his war horse, never mounted except for buffalo hunting or for battle. Marcy once made an effort to buy a favorite horse from a chief, but without

luck: "He said the animal was one of the fleetest.
. . . If he were to sell him it would prove a calamity
to his whole band, as it often required all the speed
of this animal to insure success in the buffalo chase;
that his loss would be felt by all his people, and
he would be regarded as very foolish; moreover, he
said, patting his favorite upon the neck, 'I love him
very much.' "

CHAPTER II

ARROW, LANCE, AND GUN

"THE wealth of the Indians in the Mississippi valley," said Father Marquette, "consists of the skins of wild cattle." Not only their wealth, but their tools, their ornaments, their clothing, their toys, were from the buffalo: hides, bones, sinews, and hair of the buffalo were the stuff of the hundred and one articles of the Plains Indians' culture. Deerskin was the only article that approached rivalry.

The trimming, the sewing, and the shaping were not man's work, of course. "The men go, from time to time, to hunt," wrote Father Binneteau of the Illinois Indians, "and spend the rest of the time in gaming, dancing, singing *partisque fruuntur*. They are all gentlemen." But the women—to quote another Jesuit Father,[1] who dated his letter from "Cascaskias, an Illinois village, otherwise called the Immaculate Conception of the Blessed Virgin"—were busied in working up the hair of the buffalo, "mak-

[1] R. G. Thwaites, editor, *Jesuit Relations* (72 vols): *Relation* of Marquette, LIX; *Relation* of Binneteau, LXV; *Relation* of Marest, LXVI.

ing it into leggings, girdles, and bags; for the oxen here are very different from those of Europe; besides having a great hump on the back, near the shoulders, they are also wholly covered with a fine wool, which takes the place of that which our savages would obtain from sheep, were there any in that country. The women thus occupied by work are thereby more disposed to accept the truths of the Gospel." Perhaps; but as a counterpoise to piety the women of the southern tribes made beaded strings of buffalo hair, which they wore in prophecy of garters.

The tepees of the buffalo-hunting tribes were made of hides, dressed, and sewn together; within, the tepees were supported by twenty or thirty poles. These lodges could be taken down and packed into bundles in a few minutes by the squaws; indeed, they had to be, for a tribe generally moved six or eight times in the course of one summer, to keep within reach of the roaming herds. The poles of the lodge, fastened into two bundles, were the framework for packing. A village of five or six hundred tepees, moving to find the herds and encamp about them, might be strung out in the march for miles, with the men, mounted on good horses, preceding a caravan of horses and dogs dragging the bundles, and among them and flanking them women, children, and more dogs.

On the upper Missouri, among the red-clay bluffs, the Mandans, the "people-of-the-pheasants," lived in permanent lodges—spacious cabins that held from twenty to forty persons, a family and all its connections. Their beds were of buffalo skin, stretched on posts about two feet from the ground. The fur side was uppermost, making a luxurious underblanket, and on this the Mandan slept with a folded-over buffalo robe for a pillow, and other buffalo robes for covering. And they were curtained by other buffalo skins, screened on an upright frame. In the southern range were the Comanche Indians, even more dependent on the buffalo: "They are a brave vagrant tribe," reads an early account, "and never reside but a few days in a place, but travel north with the buffalo in the summer, and, as winter comes on, return with them to the plains west of Texas."

A buffalo robe was the Indian's winter cloak by day, and his covering by night. The Osage Indians whom Lieutenant Cutler described "wear a breech flap fastened around the waist with a belt; a pair of leggins, and shoes or moccasons. They are made of dressed buffaloe or deer skin, and fancifully worked and ornamented with lead, and porcupine quills, stained with different colors." This was the common dress of the Plains Indians; only the ornamentation regularly varied, and each tribe interwove porcupine

quills according to its own designs into the ceremonial robes. One ornate Arapahoe robe was figured
with porcupine quills, red and yellow splinters inter-
mixed in the pattern, and the border of the robe
entirely hung with the hooves of young fawns, that
as the chief walked clattered like rattlesnake buttons.

The dress of that head chief of the Blackfeet
whom Catlin painted was surmounted with the robe
of a young buffalo bull; and on the smooth side,
handsomely fringed and ornamented with porcupine
quills, the battles of his life were recounted in pictures. His headdress was an ermine base for a pair
of buffalo horns polished to a fine glaze. This headdress of curving horns was an honor for the chief
alone.

The Indian's shield was commonly made of the
toughened rawhide of the bull's neck, dried by
smoke, and hardened with glue boiled from buffalo
hooves. It was only a light weight on the left arm;
but it was arrowproof, and, turned obliquely, it
deflected the shot of the old smoothbore rifles.

Bows were usually made of wood, but the best
and strongest were made of pieces of bone and horn
—buffalo, elk, or mountain sheep—spliced and
glued together, and wrapped with sinews of buffalo.
Strands of buffalo sinew made the bowstrings. The
handles of lances were roughened by a sinew wrap-
ping. The quivers and bow cases were often made

of the skin of a buffalo calf. Knives were made of the dorsal ribs of the buffalo, rubbed to a keen edge.

The place of the buffalo in Indian legend and ritual is explained by the intimate everyday importance of "the monarch of the plains" in Indian life. "The Blackfeet ask, 'What one of all animals is the most sacred?' And the reply given is, 'The Buffalo.'"

Especially with those tribes who lived in permanent lodges for at least a part of the year, a buffalo hunt was a ceremonial affair, and needed "medicine" to insure its success.

The Mandans, in their hunting excursions after buffalo, usually stayed a week or ten days, and returned on foot, their horses laden with meat and robes. But sometimes the herds had retreated far from the Mandan villages; these Indians were a small tribe, and afraid to carry the chase into the hunting range of powerful enemies. In such an emergency, the chiefs and shamans decided on the old expedient, the buffalo dance; and the criers proclaimed the decision through the village. Each man brought his mask, the head and horns of a buffalo; and the buffalo dance began. In the open space before the "mystery" lodge, ten or fifteen braves, each in his mask, and in his hand his favorite bow or lance, carried on the dance. Catlin saw a buffalo

BISON DANCE OF THE MANDAN INDIANS

From *Illustrations to Maximilian, Prince of Weid's Travels in the Interior of North America* (Ackermann & Company, London, 1844).

dance which went on for several days: "When one becomes fatigued of the exercise, he signifies it by bending quite forward, and sinking his body towards the ground; when another draws a bow upon him and hits him with a blunt arrow, and he falls like a buffalo—is seized by the bystanders, who drag him out of the ring by the heels, brandishing their knives about him; and having gone through the motions of skinning and cutting him up, they let him off, and his place is at once supplied by another, who dances into the ring with his mask on; and by this taking of places, the scene is easily kept up night and day, until the desired effect has been produced, that of 'making buffalo come.'"

In the ritual of the Manitari tribe for success in the hunt, the whole tribe assembled in the mystery lodge; six of the old men had been chosen to represent buffalo bulls; they had sticks which they rattled incessantly, ornamented with bells and calf hooves; they sang, and between songs imitated the hoarse bellowing of the buffalo bull. Dishes of boiled maize and beans were passed about by provision bearers, each man tasting a little; then empty dishes were passed about, and each man tasted those, in silent anticipation of the buffalo for which these dishes were reserved. There followed speeches of hope for success in hunt and war.

Prince Maximilian was permitted to attend one of

these ceremonies: "We also exerted ourselves in uttering good wishes in the English and German languages, which the Indians guessed from our emotions, though they could not understand our words. If our speech was lengthy, they were specially gratified; the provision bearer stopped, listened very attentively, nodded his satisfaction, and passed his hand over our right arm from the shoulder to the wrist, and sometimes over both arms, and then again spoke a few words expressive of his thanks. In this manner the ceremony of the repast lasted above an hour; every person present partook of it, and offered up their good wishes for a successful buffalo chase." The ceremony of passing the pipe succeeded "with various superstitious manœuvres." And the six actors again "stood up, bent forward, and danced; that is, they leaped as high as they could with both their feet together, continuing to sing and rattle their sticks, one of them beating time on the badger (drum). Their song was invariably the same, consisting of loud, broken notes and exclamations." Every step in the dance and every exclamation in the song had its intricate and mysterious meaning.

A creeping line of Indians encircling a herd, and at a signal suddenly facing the buffaloes with a complete wall of spears and bows—that, the simplest kind of a "surround," is doubtless the oldest way of hunting buffalo for the tribe.[2] As White Hawk, the old Cheyenne, recounted his people's history to George Bird Grinnell: "In those days the arrowpoint was made of stone. There were birds, and so they got feathers for their arrows in order that they should fly straight. Men were always out from camp looking for food. When any of these men found a herd of buffalo, twenty or thirty or forty, he returned to the camp and reported to the chief. Then all who had bows and arrows made ready, and went with these men to near where the buffalo were, and there formed a big circle as far as possible from the buffalo, but entirely surrounding them. The side of the circle to the leeward of the buffalo, and the other two sides across the wind were formed first. The windward side was formed last. Then the men began to close in on the buffalo, until, as the circle grew smaller, the hunters were closer together. When the buffalo began to smell the people, they ran away; but those toward whom they ran would

[2] Of the many excellent narratives which recount Indian hunts of buffalo, these in particular will repay reading: John Bradbury, *Travels in the Interior of America* (Ed. by R. G. Thwaites, *Early Western Travels,* Vol. V); *Original Journals of the Lewis and Clark Expedition* (preferably in the Thwaites edition: New York, 1904); Nicholas Perrot, *The Indian Tribes of the Upper Mississippi Valley* (Ed. by E. H. Blair, Cleveland, 1911); Prince Maximilian, *Travels in the Interior of North America,* Lloyd, tr. (Thwaites, *op. cit.,* Vols. XXII-XXIV); and the narratives, cited in the following pages, of Edwin James and T. J. Farnham. See also the splendid first volume of G. B. Grinnell's *The Cheyenne Indians* (New Haven, 1923).

yell and toss their robes, and the buffalo turned, looking for another place, and from being always turned back they were soon running in a circle. When the hunters got pretty close, all of the most active young men—those who had strong arms to pull the bow, and who could shoot straightest—ran in close to the buffalo and began shooting their arrows at them, while the buffalo were running round in a circle, not trying to break through the line of the people. The old men say that in this way they sometimes killed a whole herd, none of them breaking out. At times a few would break out and get away, but often all were killed. The people had dogs, and when the buffalo were skinned and cut up, they packed meat on their dogs, and then every man, woman, and child able to walk carried a pack to camp. They left nothing behind, but carried everything in. Even the bones . . . for buffalo were hard to get and were had only occasionally, and the people felt that nothing was to be wasted or left behind."

The great heaps of buffalo bones that puzzled early explorers were the débris of these surrounds.

In 1822 General Ashley, the head of the Rocky Mountain Fur Company, traveling with his company up the Platte Valley, arrived at a Pawnee Loup village. Here the traders bought some fresh horses and were ready to move on, but Two Axe, the chief, objected: "My men are about to surround the buffalo; if you go now, you will frighten them. You must stay four days more, then you may go on." And the party waited.

At least a thousand Indians took part in the hunt. They encompassed a large meadow where a herd was grazing, and closed in to form a complete circle. Two Axe's order to charge was passed down the line with telepathic speed; and in one concerted rush the Indians closed in. The slaughter did not take long; fourteen hundred buffalo were killed. "The tongues were counted by General Ashley himself," Jim Beckwourth would add by way of convincing his hearers.

The *piskun* was surer and safer than the human trap; it was an enclosed pen into which the buffalo were driven.

One side of the trap used by the Blackfeet was formed by the vertical wall of a bluff; the other sides, six or eight feet high, were built of logs, rocks, and brush. These walls did not have to be very strong, but they had to be tight enough that the buffalo could not see through them. From a point on the plateau overlooking the enclosure, piles of rock or clumps of bushes, placed at short intervals, extended outward like the outer ribs of a fan. The Indian who decoyed the buffalo into this V was usually the owner of a talisman, a "buffalo rock." The previous night he had called upon the sun and upon all Above People for power, and had burned sweet grasses to them. Early in the morning he left his lodge and went out on the prairie toward the buffalo; other Indians followed him, and hid behind the rocks and bushes which made the wings of the chute. When the decoy's antics had brought the buffalo within the V, the braves sprang up, and with shouts and robe waving stampeded the buffalo into a full run up the chute, over the bluff, and into the pen. The squaws and children were on the other side of the walls, whooping up a racket to keep the buffalo from pushing against the walls and escaping. Spears, arrows, knives did the rest; and after nightfall white-wing squads of wolves and coyotes were cleaning the pen.

The Plains Crees, about the Qu'Appelle River, where there was much timber but no rocks, built a circular pen of tree trunks lashed together with green withes and braced by prop logs. Just under the gap in the circle the ground was sharply cut out, making a wall high enough to hold the buffalo from doubling back. Two rows of bushes, the wings of the chute, extended four miles out into the prairie. A herd of buffalo, decoyed into the chute by several Indians waving buffalo robes, plunged into the circle; and the shouts of excited, exultant Indians mingled with the bellowing, moaning, and roaring of wounded and dying animals.

The Assiniboines built an enclosure in the open prairie. The fence was about four feet high and formed of strong stakes of birchwood, wattled with birch branches. The decoys were dressed in buffalo skins. "Their faces were covered, and their gestures so closely resembled those of the animals themselves," declared an explorer, "that if I had not been in the secret, I should have been as much deceived as the oxen." As soon as the buffalo had been enticed within the pen, a screen of buffalo skins on a drop cord was let down across the opening.

The Cheyenne decoys were painted from scalp to moccasins with red earth; waving eagles' wings and singing sacred songs helped them to entice the buffalo.

Some northern tribes killed buffalo by driving the herd over a high bluff—too wanton a massacre to be called a hunt. By 1820 the Cree Indians had despoiled the Sturgeon River region of buffalo by such methods as this, and had moved down into the buffalo range of the Blackfeet, who became their implacable enemies.

When the Lewis and Clark expedition, progressing up the Missouri, had just passed the mouth of the Judith River, Captain Lewis wrote in his *Journal:* "Today we passed on the Star^d. side the remains of a vast many mangled carcasses of Buffalow which had been driven over a precipice of 120 feet by the Indians and perished; the water appeared to have washed away a part of this immence pile of slaughter and still their remained the fragments of at least a hundred carcasses they created a most horrid stench. in this manner the Indians of the Missouri distroy vast herds of buffalo at a stroke; for this purpose one of the most active and fleet young men is scelected and disguised in a robe of buffaloe skin, having also the skin of the buffaloe's head with the years and horns fastened on his head in the form of a cap, thus caparisoned he places himself at a convenient distance between a herd of buffaloe and a precipice proper for the purpose, which happens in many places on this river for miles together; the other indians now surround the herd on the back and flanks and at a signal agreed on shew themselves at the same time moving forward towards the buffaloe; the disguised indian or decoy has taken care to place himself sufficiently nigh the buffaloe to be noticed by them when they take to flight and running before them they follow him in full speed to the precipice." The only pleasant feature of this way of hunting is that sometimes the decoy was not quick enough in getting out of the way.

The Indians of the upper Mississippi country had

permanent lodges, and cultivated maize, kidney-beans, and squashes. "If they are without these," said Nicholas Perrot, "they think that they are fasting, no matter what abundance of meat and fish they may have in their stores, the Indian corn being to them what bread is to Frenchmen." But as long as buffalo were abundant in their region, every autumn, after the harvest had been gathered, and again in early summer, after the grain had been planted, the tribes set out for the buffalo range. All the Indians in a village went together to the hunt; and if there were not enough, two or three villages united. Without horses, a few men could not hope to cope with a herd of several hundred buffalo.

One of the prominent war chiefs was made commander of the expedition; "dog soldiers," or policemen of the hunt, were appointed, and the assembled Indians were reinstructed in the code of the chase. Nothing must be permitted which might stampede the buffalo and ruin the prospects of the hunt. The disobedient could be deprived of their weapons, their bows and arrows broken, their cabins torn down, their property taken away; the law was inexorable, and not even the chief had special liberties.

The night before the hunting was to begin, three parties of young men were sent out, making careful marches to surround the herd. When the sun had risen high enough to dry away the dew, the young men on each flank of the herd set fire to the prairie; and at that moment the entire village broke camp, and started a fourth palisade of fire. The old men, squaws, and boys kept up a confusing clamor until, as the lines of fire met each other, the buffalo were completely enclosed. Then the braves twanged arrows into the crowded, panic-stricken herd until, perhaps, not one buffalo was left. Elk and deer caught within these circles dashed across the rim, and escaped; a prairie fire was not a thick blaze, but only a thin line of flame. Buffaloes raced along that line, not daring the one jump that would have cleared them of the flames and given them a chance of escape.

In their winter hunts, when snows made the surround-by-fire impossible, these Indians of the upper Mississippi had to form a palisade of men; unless several villages united to make a closely packed line, there was not the same chance of success, and some danger to the braves.

In the rugged districts of the northern range, winds blew the snow from the high places and banked up drifts in the hollows and ravines. Indian hunters, on snowshoes, drove the buffalo from the plateaus; and once in the drifts, the heavy beasts floundered helplessly until the hunter caught up, and jammed home his lance. A thick crust upon the snow gave the hunter the same advantage. The

HUNTING ON SNOW SHOES

From George Catlin, *North American Indian Portfolio* (George Catlin, London, n. d.).

Manitari Indians drove in light sledges pulled by dogs, into the midst of the herd; the hunter simply sat in his sledge and let fly his arrows.

As mustangs became common to the tribes, and all Indians but the very poorest owned at least one horse, hunting the buffalo was much easier than in the old days, and medicine men lost prestige because their services were no longer necessary to bring the buffalo. The walls of the enclosures were allowed to crumble, and the old habit of burning the prairie was given up.

In 1820 Major Long's expedition was among the Omahas, and Edwin James, the narrator of the expedition, made careful notes of their way of life.

On Omaha Creek, within two or three miles of the Missouri, the tribe had a permanent village of earth lodges. Here they came in April, and the squaws planted maize, beans, pumpkins, melons, and dressed the buffalo robes from the last winter's hunt, while the young men set beaver traps and hunted other furred animals in the near-by country.

In June, when provisions had begun to fail, the chiefs assembled a council. The indispensable ceremony of smoking was the first course in the dinner, speeches came next, and the dog fricassee last. The principal chief, after giving thanks to each chief and brave by name for the pleasure of his company, raised the question of the route the hunting party should take: up the Niobrara, up the Platte, or into the plain between the two streams. Again, the question might be raised if there were not enough maize on hand to support the tribe in pleasant inactivity until the fall; or if the warriors should not make a long foray into the southwest to capture wild horses. And discussion continued until the camp criers took the kettles from the fire, and offered a spoonful of the soup to each of the four cardinal points and a fifth to the "Great Wahconda." Feasting followed, and smoking again.

"The criers now sing through the village in praise of the host, thanking him before the people for his hospitality, repeating also the names of the chiefs who were present, and thanking them for their kindness to the old criers, who, they say, are disqualified by age from any other occupations than those of eating, smoking, and talking; they also communicate to the people the resolutions of the council." And the squaws made ready for the expedition, mending moccasins and robes, preparing the pack-saddles and the dog sleds, and making a *cache* in the earth for all the property that was not to be taken with them. "The men in the mean time amuse themselves with hunting, playing with the hoop and stick, cards, dancing; whilst at night the young warriors and beaux are occupied with affairs of gallantry, or contriving assignations." And when the day of departure had arrived, the squaws loaded the horses and dogs, threw piles of brushwood against the closed entrances to the lodges, and shouldered their own packs; the tribe left a completely deserted village.

In this year the party had to travel, at its pedestrian pace, fifteen or twenty days before the scouts located a large herd. When from some elevation the sign was given that many buffalo were just ahead, the Omahas unpacked their skin tepees and encamped. The chiefs of the hunt assumed command; dog soldiers were appointed, painted themselves black, and paraded the camp armed with clubs or thongs. The old criers made the round of the tepees, "requesting the squaws to keep in good heart, telling them that they have endured many hardships with fortitude, that there is now a termination of their difficulties for the present, and that on the morrow the men will go in pursuit of the bisons, and without doubt bring them plenty of meat."

Just after dawn, the braves rode out to the chase. A pipe bearer, afoot, preceded them and the dog soldiers walked beside the mounted hunters. Once in sight of the herd the hunters gave kindly advice to their horses, not to fear the bison, to run well, and not to be gored. The pipe bearer blew puffs of smoke toward the heavens, the four winds, the earth, and the buffalo. Then the chief gave the word; and two lines of hunters passed at full speed toward the right and left of the herd. In this quick chase the hunter must be clever at placing his arrows and sure in his horsemanship for notable success.

A fleet, well-trained horse ran, without guidance from his rider, apace with the buffalo, turned as the buffalo turned, and did not slacken his run until the bowstring had twanged. Then, at the sway of his rider, he was at full gallop again, beside another buffalo. The best of these mustangs were as hardy as they were spirited. Alexander Henry had a gray horse he had bought from the Mandans: one day Henry chased a hart five miles before he caught up and killed him; an hour afterwards he started a large meadow hare, and shot it only after a long chase; toward evening he ran down a herd of buffalo and killed a fat cow for his supper; and although he had ridden about thirty miles that day, besides these excursions after game, the little mustang showed no sign of fatigue.

"Whilst in full run," wrote Edwin James of the Omaha hunters, "they discharge the arrow with an aim of much certainty, so that it penetrates the body of the animal behind the shoulder. If it should not bury itself so deeply as they wish, they are often known to ride up to the enraged animal and withdraw it. They observe the direction and depth to which the arrow enters, in order to ascertain whether or not the wound is mortal, of which they can judge with a considerable degree of exactness; when a death-wound is inflicted, the hunter raises a shout of exultation, to prevent others from pursuing the individual of which he considers himself certain. He then passes in pursuit of another, and so on, until his quiver is exhausted, or the game has passed beyond his further pursuit."

The summer hunt continued for about two months, the tepees packed again and moved to another camp site as the buffalo in one locality were killed or driven away. In August the Omahas returned to their village, with quantities of dried meat and summer skins. The *caches* were opened and the goods put back in the lodges; the squaws cleared away the weeds; the maize was harvested, and dried or pounded; and the pumpkins were shredded and dried. The braves contented themselves in the village until late October, when the tepees were packed again and the winter hunt, for beaver and buffalo, was begun. When there was need, a family returned to the village and uncovered its *cache* of dried food, then returned to the buffalo range about the Missouri or about the Elkhorn. When spring was well advanced, the Omahas left off this nomadic life and sifted back into the village.[3]

[3] Edwin James, *Account of an Expedition . . . to the Rocky Mountains* (Thwaites, *op. cit.,* Vols. XIV-XVII).

The wooden lance was an old-time weapon of the Plains tribes for killing buffalo. The rider usually ran up to the right side of the game, and used both hands in thrusting the lance downward and forward, for the heart, or, to cripple the animal, for the kidneys. When arrow points of iron succeeded stone points, the lances were also given a blade of iron.

The Comanches used the bow and arrow or the lance indifferently. For many years after guns were introduced among the Indians, the use of arrow, lance, or gun was largely a matter of preference and of social rank. The chiefs were especially reluctant to cast off tradition and use guns; the killing of many buffalo seemed a greater personal feat if one of the old-time weapons was used. Among the Kansas Indians, whom Thomas Farnham met on their spring hunt in 1839, "the high chief has a lance, with a handle six feet and a blade three feet in length. This in hand . . . he rides boldly to the side of the flying buffalo, and thrusts it again and again through the liver or heart of one and then another of the affrighted herd until his horse is no longer able to keep near them. Some of the inferior chiefs also have these lances; but they must all be shorter than that of his Royal Darkness. The common Indians use muskets and pistols. Rifles are an abomination to them. The twisting motion of the ball as it enters, the sharp crack when discharged, and the direful singing of the lead as it cuts the air, are considered symptoms of witchcraft that are unsafe for the Indian to meddle with. . . . The poorer classes still use the bow and arrow." [4]

Out of bravado or necessity, hunters have used strange ways and strange weapons to kill buffalo. Big Ribs, a Northern Cheyenne, once rode close beside a large bull, sprang from his horse to the buffalo, rode some distance, then leaned over and buried his knife into the flank of the buffalo. Big Ribs, incidentally, and another Cheyenne, Strong Left Hand, are each credited with having shot one arrow through two buffaloes and killing both. Father de Smet once met seven Flathead Indians just returned from a hunt; they had killed one hundred and eighty-nine buffalo. One of these Flatheads had distinguished himself with three remarkable hits. Armed merely with a stone, he had pursued a cow, and on the run he had thrown the stone between the cow's horns, fatally; afterwards he had killed a second with his knife; and after crippling a large bull with a spear thrust, he had finished the job by strangling him. The Abbé Domenech, a trusting soul lacking one grain of skepticism, relates that sometimes "a courageous unhorsed rider continues on foot the struggle he began on horseback, while

[4] T. J. Farnham, *Travels in the Great Western Prairie* (Thwaites, *op. cit.,* Vol. XXVIII).

he is attacked on every side. . . . But Indians are inured to these hand to hand combats, and wait fearlessly until the animal is near enough for the hunter to blindfold it with a belt or any other piece of leather; and while the poor beast tries to get rid of the muffle, it receives an arrow or a knife deep in its body, close to its heart." Captain Bonneville's journal told of his seeing a hunting party of Indians and half-breeds "who amused themselves with a grotesque kind of buffalo bait. Whenever they found a huge bull in the plains, they prepared for their teasing and barbarous sport. Surrounding him on horseback, they would discharge their arrows at him in quick succession, goading him to make an attack; which, with a dexterous movement of the horse, they would easily avoid. In this way they hovered round him, feathering him with arrows, as he reared and plunged about, until he was all bristled over like a porcupine. When they perceived in him signs of exhaustion, and he could no longer be provoked to make battle, they would dismount from their horses, approach him in the rear, and seizing him by the tail, jerk him from side to side, and drag him backward, until the frantic animal would break from them."

When bows and arrows alone were used, each brave, knowing his own arrows, could easily identify his own kill. If, of two arrows in the body of a buffalo, the braves concerned could not decide which had been the fatal shot, the principal chief made a decision; but an appeal could be taken to the general judgment of the dog soldiers. After the general use of firearms made such identification impossible, the division became more of a communistic affair, and the meat and skins were divided by some rule of the tribe's invention.

"The Indian is a great epicure," said Colonel Richard Dodge; "knows the choicest tidbits of every animal, and how to cook it to suit his taste. The great fall hunt yields to him the fullest enjoyment of his appetite." *Epicure* is too delicately flavored a word; the Indian was an enthusiast at eating, not an artist.

As soon as the hunt was over, the lucky warrior cut open his buffalo, and helped himself to a raw repast. The smaller entrails usually went first, then the liver, perhaps another organ or two. The liver of a fat buffalo sometimes became granulated by the heat of a long chase; this, with the gall bladder burst over it, was esteemed beyond all other morsels.

The *dépouille* was a fat substance lying along the backbone, next to the hide, running from the shoulder blade to the last rib. This was stripped out and dipped in hot grease for half a minute, then hung up inside the lodge to dry and smoke for a day. "It will keep indefinitely, and is used as a substitute for bread," a frontiersman described it, "but is superior to any bread that was ever made."

The tongues, roasted or boiled fresh, or cured by steeping in cold water, then in tepid water, and salt then rubbed into them, and the roasted marrow-bones, were the parts of the buffalo most relished by traders and travelers.

Buffalo meat that was to be dried was cut into thin slices, wound about sticks which slanted over a slow fire, or laid upon a rick of wickerwork. Sometimes the heat of the sun alone was enough for drying. To make pemmican, these dried-out slices were pounded into a flaky mass; over successive layers of these shreds an equal weight, or almost so, of fat which had been melted and was yet soft, was poured. Buffalo fat was far more palatable stuff than is the fat of domestic oxen, and any quantity, plainsmen said, could be eaten without fear of indigestion; so that this layer loaf of alternate meat and fat, packed in bags made of buffalo skin, was nutritious, compact food, capable of being kept indefinitely, and acceptable if not exciting to the taste. Pemmican became the standard food of the fur traders.

Buffalo robes—the winter skin of the buffalo, when his coat of hair was at its blackest, thick, and handsome—were dressed by the squaws to be acceptable in commerce. The fur traders never bought untanned robes; no white men could attain the exquisite workmanship of the Indians. The method of dressing the robes varied somewhat among the tribes. The Crow Indians were probably the most careful of all. No tribe, Catlin thought, could match in beauty the work of the Crow squaws. First they immersed the buffalo hide in a mixture of ashes and water for a few days, that loosened away the hair; next they pinned the skin taut to the ground, with tapering stakes through the edges, and shampooed the skin with handfuls of the brains of buffalo. The women then dried and thinned the skin by graining it with a sharpened bone, usually the shoulder blade of the buffalo. There was a final process of smoking the skins, that gave them the quality of drying soft and pliant whenever rain fell upon them.

A white buffalo—so great a rarity that even the Great Spirit must have been surprised when one was born—received its due meed of awe from most Plains tribes. To the Mandans especially the skin of a white buffalo was fine medicine, and a good white skin would bring the price of ten or fifteen horses. Three or four years after the purchase, piety demanded that the skin be offered to the dessication of wind and rain.

CHAPTER III

AROUND the salt springs of Big Bone Lick, Kentucky, there lie, ten feet below the surface and extending to an unknown depth, the remains of great elephants, their skeletons broken into pieces by the tread of successive generations who have come to drink the salty water. Above that level lie the remains of a musk ox, once forced into this southern country by the march of the great glacier, together with the remains of a long-extinct species of bison. After the elephant and the mastodon, after smaller game had come to these springs and sunk in the mire and their kind had been forgotten—at the very subsurface of the springs—are the bones of the American bison.

Long before the Pueblo Indians came into New Mexico, a citizen of a primitive Three Rivers, New Mexico, hammered the outline of a buffalo into the rock wall of his cave. But it was probably on the very eve of the last disastrous battle with the northern invaders that a Mound Builder stripped the last bite of meat from the thigh bone of a buffalo, and threw the bone atop a pile of kitchen débris. In all the Mounds, in all the relics of the hunts and feasts of the Mound Builders who lived east of Illinois, that thigh bone, in the top layer of a midden near Muskingum, Ohio, is the only presence of buffalo. The West was the natural dominion of the buffalo; it was not until, say, the year 1000 that the buffalo herds crossed the Mississippi.

But were the Mound Builders exterminated in battle or did their agrarian culture vanish with the coming of the buffalo herds? Nathaniel Shaler, attempting forty years ago to balance the equation of nature and man in America, hazarded: "These tribes appear, after the coming of the buffalo, to have lapsed into the pure savagery which hunting entails. To favor the pasturage of these wild herds, the Indians adopted the habit of burning the prairies. These fires spread to the forests in the east, killing the young trees . . . extending the pasturage area of the wild herds until the larger portions of the westward plains eastward to central Ohio and Kentucky . . . had been stripped of their original forests, making way for the vast throngs of these creatures." [1]

When the first settlers came into Kentucky a great area was unwooded—"The Barrens," supposed to be worthless; but this space had been

[1] N. S. Shaler, *Nature and Man in America* (New York, 1891).

burned away by the Indians, probably by the Shawnee tribe, to offer an enticing pasturage to the great game animals of the Plains. Centuries of repeated firing are necessary to deforest such an area of its beech and ash; here six thousand square miles had been made into a treeless plain. As soon as the regular hunting incursions of the Indians were stopped, "The Barrens" speedily sprang up into forest again. This willful firing, to extend the grazing area of the buffalo herds, must account for part of the deforestation of the prairie lands of Indiana and Illinois.[2]

The eastward extension of the buffalo range stopped short of the seaboard, except, probably, in the Georgia lowlands near Savannah. The limit was, roughly, just above the falls line of the Atlantic streams; above the Allegheny Mountains of Pennsylvania a limiting line might be drawn to the midway point of the southern shore of Lake Ontario. The earliest discovery of buffalo in the East, however, was made upon the banks of the Potomac.

[2] N. S. Shaler, *Kentucky* (Boston, 1884); J. A. Allen, "The American Bison Living and Extinct."

Cf. Journals of Lewis and Clark, March 6, 1805: "a cloudy morning & smokey all Day from the burning of the plains, which was set on fire by the *Minetarries* for an early crop of grass, as an inducement for the Buffalow to feed on. . . ."

Cf. also the suggestive analogy of the change from agrarian to hunting culture of the Cheyenne tribe: G. B. Grinnell, *The Cheyenne Indians,* Vol. I (New Haven, 1923).

HUNTING UNDER THE WHITE WOLF SKIN

From George Catlin, *North American Indian Portfolio* (George Catlin, London, n. d.).

Sir Samuel Argoll, "in a letter touching his voyage to Virginia, and actions there," relates that having sailed up that river, "and then marching into the Countrie, I found great store of Cattle as big as Kine, of which the Indians that were my guides killed a couple, which we found to be very good and wholesome meate, and are very easy to be killed, in regard they are heavy, slow, and not so wild as other beasts of the wildernesse." But the English colonists found no "great store" so near the sea-coast. The earliest colonists in New England knew of the buffalo only by vague hearsay; Thomas Morton, the convivial leader of Merrymount, in 1637 made note of "great heards of well-growne beasts" that were some distance to the west, and adds, "It is tenne yeares since first the relation of these things came to the eares of the English." And the earliest history of Carolina (1714) records of the buffalo, "He seldom appears among the English Inhabitants, his chief haunt being in the land of the Messiasippi [sic], which is for the most part a plain country; yet I have known some killed on the Hilly Part of Cape-Fair-River [that is, above the falls line], they passing the ledges of the vast Mountains from the said Messiasippi before they can come near us." Colonel William Byrd's expedition of 1729, to survey the boundary between Virginia and South Carolina, found buffalo at Sugar-Tree Creek, within a hundred and fifty-five miles of the coast; but there were none nearer.

When explorers and frontiersmen crossed the Appalachians, the favorite paths were the buffalo roads. The famous route through Cumberland Gap into Kentucky was the grassless trace of files of buffalo. The two other great routes overland across the mountains into the Middle West were first marked out by buffalo hooves: the course into northern Ohio that the New York Central follows to-day, and the course from the Potomac cross-country to the Ohio River. The great north-and-south trails of warring Indians in the Middle West followed the buffalo traces. And in the sweeping phrase of Senator Thomas Benton, the buffalo blazed the way for the railroads to the Pacific.

Where forested bits of land compressed a scattered herd into a single line, short roads were tramped out, leading to the salt licks. The buffalo so unvaryingly found their way to these licks that the earliest maps of the trans-Appalachian country carefully indicated the position of these licks, as a guide to hunters.

Kentucky was favored with many salt licks, the resorts of thousands of buffalo. "Nature seems to measure her works on a different scale on the opposite sides of the Appalachian mountains," wrote Gilbert Imlay, commissioner for laying out lands in the Back Settlements; "in speaking of a new country, that is extremely fertile and well covered with herbage, it is hardly necessary to say that it abounds in wild game. The buffalo, elk, deer, and bear are numerous (in Kentucky); nor is there any scarcity of wolves, panthers, wild-cats, foxes, beavers, and otters. They have pheasants, partridges or quails, and turkies in abundance throughout the year. During the winter, their waters are covered with the swan, wild-goose, brant, and duck. Cat-fish have been caught in those rivers, that weighed above 100 pounds, and perch that weighed above 20 pounds." No Indian nation had permanent lodges in this rich hunting ground; in the immemorial conflicts for possession of these meadows and their herds, Kentucky was a "Dark and Bloudy Ground" long before there were feuds in "them ther' " hills.

Thomas Walker, the appointee of the Loyal Land Company of England and Virginia to "go to the westward, in order to discover a proper place for settlement," was the first explorer who came beyond question of doubt into central Kentucky. "We kept . . . along the Indian road . . . A large Buffaloe Road goes from that Fork to the Creek over the West Ridge, which we took and found the Ascent and Descent tollerably easie." So read typical entries in his journal. Once, as the ex-

ploring party followed a buffalo road, it met a
buffalo bull, ready to defend his exclusive title to
the lane: "We were obliged to shoot him, or he
would have been amongst us."

About the great Salt Lick at the site of Roanoke,
Virginia, were a few settlers; here Walker, beginning his travels, bought corn for his horses. Already
hunters had thinned out the buffalo from the Blue
Ridge: "This Lick has been one of the best places
for Game in these parts & would have been of much
greater advantage to the Inhabitants than it has
been if the Hunters had not killed the Buffaloes
for diversion." As early as March 15, 1750, then,
there exists an observer's comment that wanton,
wasteful slaughter has hastened the departure of
the buffalo from a locality. Hundreds of travelers
were to write down that observation again.

The real beginnings of agriculture in Kentucky
lagged several years behind the beginnings of settlement, so easy was life by the gun. The buffalo
had not yet learned to run at the sight or smell of
man, and the hunter soon learned the trick of shooting the most wary buffalo at the edge of the herd,
of holding a herd in stupid confusion until the
number of slaughtered buffalo actually befouled the
salt spring. "I have heard a hunter assert that he
saw above 1000 buffaloes at the Blue Licks at once,"
old John Filson said, "so numerous were they be-

fore the first settlers had wantonly sported away their lives." By 1810 there were no buffalo in Kentucky.[3]

In Pennsylvania the buffalo, threading their way along hills and through forests, previsaged in their tremendous size, and the darker color and the greater curl of their hair, the development of a subspecies of wood bison, differing in many details from the buffalo of the plains, if the buffalo had survived a few more centuries. Seasonal migrations had been from the Ohio country, across western Pennsylvania, into the valleys of West Virginia; but by 1760 the wedge of settlement had cleaved this route, and northern and southern Pennsylvania each had its own herd. In 1770 there were still more than ten thousand buffalo in the northern herd; "when the persimmons became ripe along the Bald Eagle Mountains" hunters began to watch for lines of buffalo picking footway from the table-lands of the "Seven Mountains" into the valleys.

Here, in the Seven Mountains of Centre County, the last herd of buffalo in Pennsylvania took refuge; settlements to the south prevented their wintering

[3] A. B. Hurlburt, *Paths of the Mound-Building Indians and Great Game Animals* (Cleveland, 1902); Gilbert Imlay, *A Topographical Description of the Western Territory of America* (London, 1797, 3d ed.); Daniel Boone, *Narrative* . . . (bound with Imlay, *ibid.*); Fortescue Cuming, *Sketches of a Tour in the Western Country* (R. G. Thwaites, *Early Western Travels,* Vol. IV).

in the valleys, and persistent hunters in the West Branch valley to the north cut off the only other line of escape. For perhaps three years these buffalo stayed in the inaccessible table-lands, winter and summer, while the wave of settlement lapped nearer.

In December of 1799 the snow was encrusted with ice, the wind was unusually bitter; the buffalo must penetrate into the lower valleys, where the snow could be trampled into slush and grass dug out. Led by a giant coal-black bull, the herd in single file began the descent.

On the mountain slope was the farm of Martin Bergstresser. The hay crop of his first season's cutting was beside his barn, and his cattle and sheep were sidling close to the stack, when they scented the buffaloes. They broke into flight as the herd crashed through the rail fence and nosed the haystack. Bergstresser and one Samuel McClellan, a settler whose cabin was a short distance down the valley, were near by cutting wood; their guns were beside them, their dogs were with them; they rushed to the herd, and the shots and the attacks of the dogs soon terrified the buffaloes into a rush down the frozen creek bed.

McClellan started home; he found three hundred or more buffalo snorting and trampling around the lot where his cabin stood. He rushed through the mass, and found the old lead bull standing inquisitively in front of the cabin door. McClellan's wife and children were inside the cabin. The frantic man fired at the bull; the old buffalo was stung into irritation by the shot, and plunged headlong through the door of the cabin. The herd, accustomed to follow him, forced their way after. All the man outside could hear was the heavy breathing and the bumping of the buffaloes in the cabin. When Bergstresser and three other neighbors, attracted by the shots, came up, they had to tear down a side of the cabin before they could get the buffaloes out. Nothing remained of the furniture of larger size than a handspike. The bodies of McClellan's wife and his children were crushed into the earth floor.

It took two or three days for a party of about fifty hunters to be gathered. When they started after the herd, snow was falling again, and they traveled two days in the trackless valley before they found the buffalo. The animals were huddled pitifully in a hollow, the snow up to their necks, the crust and the cold holding them numb until the hunters came. Some of the men used guns, but most of them sloughed to within knife thrust of the buffalo, and cut their throats. "Three hundred buffaloes stood upright in the frozen crust, most with jaws broken, and all with tongues gone, while the ice about them resembled a sheet of crimson glass." And the hunters marched back to the lowlands, singing German hymns. The next day, the first of January, 1800, there were no buffalo in Pennsylvania.[4]

In an Ohio post—Fort Washington—General Harmar wrote to his friend Daniel Clymer, in March, 1790, inviting him westward: "We can afford you buffalo and venison in abundance," he promised. But by the end of 1802 the last buffalo in Ohio had been killed.[5]

Thomas Ashe, traveling in the West of 1805, met an old man who had lived with some companions in a log cabin near a salt spring: "In the first and second years this old man killed from 600 to 700 buffalo . . . merely for the sake of their skins, which to them were worth only two shillings each; and after this 'work of death' they were obliged to leave the place until the following season; or till the wolves, bears, panthers, eagles, rooks, ravens, etc., had devoured the carcasses, and abandoned the place for other prey." In the two following years these same hunters killed some buffalo of the first herds that came to the lick, and—of course—left the carcasses exposed; "but they soon had reason to repent of this; for the remaining droves, as they

[4] Henry W. Shoemaker, *A Pennsylvania Bison Hunt* (Middleburg, Pa., 1915).

[5] Alfred T. Goodman, "Memo. and Notes: the Buffalo in Ohio," *Western Reserve Historical Society Tract No. 36* (January 1877).

CHASING BACK

From George Catlin, *North American Indian Portfolio* (George Catlin, London, n. d.).

came up in succession, stopped, gazing on the mangled and putrid bodies, sorrowfully moaned or furiously lowed aloud, and returned instantly, without tasting their favorite spring . . . nor did they, nor any of their race, ever revisit the neighborhood."

The simple history of that spring was repeated wherever the early geographers had marked on their maps the symbol for "Salt Springs & Licks." And the canebrakes about the creeks were fired, the buffalo killed as they were driven out. Ashe met one settler who had killed two thousand buffalo, not a bad record for a hunter in a country that numbered its buffalo by hundreds, against the hundred thousands of the trans-Mississippi West.[6]

Michaux in 1802 met one of these hunters, embarked in a canoe on the Ohio and headed for the banks of the Missouri, which he knew were luxuriant with beaver and buffalo. "His costume, like that of all American sportsmen, consisted of a waistcoat with sleeves, a pair of pantaloons, and a large red and yellow worsted sash. A carabine, a tomahawk . . . two beaver-snares, and a large knife suspended at his side, constituted his sporting-dress." [7]

There were then, Michaux estimated, three thou-

---

[6] Thomas Ashe, *Travels in America* (London, 1808).
[7] F. A. Michaux, *Travels to the West of the Alleghany Mountains* (Thwaites, *op. cit.,* Vol. III), pp. 192-193.

sand Americans about the banks of the Missouri, scattered as far as two hundred and fifty miles from the confluence with the Mississippi. Beaver pelts for profit, and buffalo meat for subsistence, was the lure. It was a time of optimism in the fur trade; the eastern streams had been thinned of beaver, but tales were common of the great plenty of many kinds of fur-bearing animals in the West. And as for buffalo meat, something has already been said of its place in the gourmanderie of the savage. The importance of this food in the fur trade is no less striking; and the intrigues of French adventurers with Indians incidentally affected the art of the kettle, bringing new savors into western cooking. There is no better introduction to the fur traders' West than the description of the *boudin blanc* by Captain Meriwether Lewis in the immortal *Journal* he shared with William Clark.

"From the buffalo cow I killed we saved the necessary materials for making what our wrighthand cook Charbono calls the *boudin* (*poudinge*) *blanc,* and immediately set him about preparing them for supper; this white pudding we all esteem one of the greatest delicacies of the forest. . . . About six feet of the lower extremity of the large gut of the buffaloe is the first morsel that the cook makes love to, this he holds fast at one end with the right hand, while with the forefinger and thumb of his left he gently compresses it and discharges what he says *is not good to eat,* but of which in the sequal we get a moderate portion; the mustle lying beneath the shoulder blade to the back, and fillets, are next saught, these are needed up very fine with a good portion of kidney suit; to this composition is then added a just proportion of pepper and salt and a small quantity of flour; thus far advanced, our skil-full operator C———o seizes his receptacle, which has never once touched water, for that would in-tirely distroy the regular order of the whole proce-dure; you will not forget that this side you see now is that covered with a good coat of fat provided the animal be in good order; the opporater sceizes the receptacle I say, and tying it fast at one end turns it inward and begins anew with repeated evolutions of the hand and arm, and a brisk motion of his finger and thumb to put in what he says is *bon pour manger;* thus by stuffing and compressing he soon distends the receptacle to the utmost limits of its power of expansion . . . thus when the sides of the receptacle are skilfully exchanged the outer for the inner . . . it is tied at the end, but not any cut off, for that would make the pattern too scant; it is then baptised in the missouri with two dips and a flirt, and bobbed into the kettle; from whence, after it be well boyled it is taken and fryed with bears oil until it becomes brown."

CHAPTER IV

THE RED RIVER VALLEY

IN the summer of 1800 Alexander Henry,[1] for the Northwest Fur Company, led *voyageurs* and Indian hunters on a trading expedition to the Saulteur Indians about the Forks of the Red River of the North—with five hundred pounds of merchandise, and guns, knives, and tobacco, and ninety gallons of "high wine," to be translated into beaver skins, bear skins, other furs, and into pemmican.

"I found forty Saulteurs awaiting my arrival; they were provided with a plentiful stock of dried buffalo meat, and anxious for a dram. I accordingly gave liquor in return for their provisions; they fell to and kept drinking all night, during which we were plagued by mosquitoes, and prevented from sleeping by the howling which the Indians and the dogs kept up."

By late August the great plain of the Red River was lush with buffaloes completing their desultory migration southward. Indian hunters riding ahead

[1] *The Manuscript Journals of Alexander Henry* [the Younger] *and of David Thompson* (3 vols.: New York, 1897), ed. by Elliott Coues.

of Henry's party left heaps of buffalo meat upon the meadow for the *voyageurs* who followed. Henry, an amateur at the sport, hunted with beginner's luck. He and his companion rode out from camp and found a buffalo resting in the tall grass. They dismounted, and crawled within thirty paces of the bull. "I desired my companion, who was an old buffalo hunter, to fire at him as he lay; this he declined, as buffalo can seldom be shot dead in that posture; he begged me to start the bull with a shot, when he would be ready to fire. I aimed as best I could for the heart, and let fly—when behold! The bull fell on his side, stretched out his legs, neck, and tail, and instantly expired—to my own great satisfaction, but the sad disappointment of my companion."

The Indians amused themselves for an afternoon by lying in wait under the bank of the Plum River for the buffalo to come to drink. When the thirsty brutes came within ten yards of the stream, a volley of twenty-five guns was fired into them. Some that were wounded dragged themselves away; the many that fell were left for the wolves and crows—the hunters wanted only the tongues.

On the Red River, near the entrance of its salt-water tributary, the Park, Henry built a trading post. Because of the briny smack of the Park water, the banks were much frequented by game—buffalo, elk, moose, bears, raccoons; and wolves were "numerous and insolent." In September buffalo grazed in immense herds on the plain below the post. When Henry and his French Canadian companion first reached this plain, the Bois Perce, they crawled through the grass to within gunshot, and opened fire. At the report of each shot the buffalo would look up from their grazing, but did not appear inclined to run off. Both hunters emptied their powder horns, and had brought several cows to the ground, before the herd took alarm and moved away. And to the mortification of the hunters the wounded cows jumped up and trotted away with the rest.

At every bend of the Red River westward, where the plains ran down to the water, the banks were grooved and worn down by the buffalo. At the Bois Perce each bank of the river was a prairie's edge, and that spot was marked as a crossing place, with buffalo ruts, some of them a foot deep, converging at the smooth, hard banks.

At the Park River fort, Henry spent the winter, trading with the Saulteur and the Red Lake Indians. There was always a group of Indians about his post, with the brawling and drunkenness that the fur trade began and nurtured. Henry's journal for the winter takes casual notice of excesses and accidents: "On the nineteenth some of the Red Lake

Indians, having traded here for liquor which they took to their camp, quarreled among themselves. Cautoquoince jumped on Terre Grasse, and bit his nose off. It was some time before the piece could be found, but at last, by tumbling and tossing the straw about, it was recovered, stuck on, and bandaged, as best the drunken people could, in hopes it would grow again." And there were several murders—in every case originated in the liaison of jealousy and trading-company rum.

The buffalo learned fear quickly. A herd of cows going at full speed southward came to a track worn by Henry and his hunters; they sniffed the ground, and, as suddenly as if horsemen had suddenly confronted them, they galloped off to the north. Henry saw a band of buffalo bulls, traveling slowly and feeding as they went, come to a place where some of his men had recently passed on foot; the bulls instantly stopped, bellowed, and tore the earth with their horns. Sometimes the whole herd would range along the man track, noisy and bewildered, until one of them was hardy enough to jump over; then the rest followed at a run.

In mid-January the plains about the post were covered with buffalo moving slowly northward. The ice-bound river was black with them. At daybreak on the fourteenth Henry was awakened by their bellowing. He climbed an oak for a better view. "The ground was covered at every point of the compass, as far as the eye could reach, and every animal was in motion. All hands attacked them with a tremendous running fire, which put them to a quicker pace, but had no effect in altering their course. The first roads beaten in the snow were followed by those in the rear. They passed at full speed until about nine o'clock, when their numbers decreased and they kept farther off in the plain." His journal for the fifteenth reads: "The plains were still covered with buffalo moving slowly northward." The entry for the sixteenth notes the passing of some lagging old bulls, the last of the herd.

Food had come literally to the gates of the post: "My winter stock of provision is complete—all good, fat buffalo meat, and my men have little to do. They, therefore, amuse themselves by sliding down the bank on sleighs from the south gate. Their descent is so great as to cause their trains to run across Red River. The Indian women join them, and they have great sport. . . . Hunting is out of the question now."

A few buffalo, "lone scabby bulls," took shelter in the woods, and the dogs about the post had sport in chasing them.

Henry, from the top of his oak, daily counted from twenty to thirty herds of buffalo feeding in the plains. Piercing north winds scraped the snow from the open field and piled it in drifts; the herds went to the woods in stormy weather, but it was no sooner abated than they faced the wind and returned to the prairie.

On the twenty-eighth of February Henry recorded: "An Indian brought in a calf of this year, which he found dead. It was well grown, and must have perished last night in the cold. This was thought extraordinary; they say it denotes an early spring." And thereafter Henry's journal seizes eagerly on each intimation of the brighter season: "On the 8th it rained for four hours; fresh meat thawed. On the 9th we saw the first spring bird. . . . My men begin to take raccoons, which are very lean. . . . On the twelfth we saw an outarde [wild goose] on the ice; and another swimming, where the melting of the snow had caused the ice to rise and leave an open space. . . . The small bastard maple begins to run. The ice is rising rapidly, in consequence of the melting snow. *20th*. I saw a sturgeon jump." By the end of March the ice was drifting in large masses, bearing great numbers of drowned buffalo from above the post. When the river was clear of ice, drowned buffaloes drifted by in herds; the carcasses formed one continuous line in the current for two days and nights.

Henry set about preparing his goods for the

canoe trip to the Grand Portage, and beyond to Montreal—making up his pemmican into bags of ninety pounds each, fifty pounds of beef and forty of tallow; and baling his furs. The canoes were ready for embarkation on the fourth of May.

In this season at the Park River, the winter of 1800-1801, Henry sent thirty-one buffalo robes to the Grand Portage. There was opportunity to have sent thousands; but red fox, black bear, and—above all else—beaver, were the furs in demand. But he sent also over five thousand pounds of pemmican. For the next eight years the Northwest Company relied on Henry for most of its pemmican.

In the summer of 1801 Alexander Henry built a post at Pembina River, in a district he called the "nursery" of the buffalo, and rich in the valuable fur-bearing animals. The Pembina post became a permanent one; and annually he sent well-laden canoes to the Grand Portage. The great trade was in beaver, of course. In his first spring at Pembina, Henry sent six hundred and twenty-nine beaver skins to the Northwest Company. In seven years he dispatched three thousand, nine hundred beaver skins, and about two thousand other furs. In these seven years the Northwest Company received from all its posts in the Lower Red River Department (the number of posts varied with the year, from four to eight) only a hundred and fifty buffalo

HERD OF BISON ON THE UPPER MISSOURI

From *Illustrations to Maximilian, Prince of Weid's Travels in the Interior of North America* (Ackermann & Company, London, 1844).

robes. One hundred of these came from Henry. In a typical year, 1805, the Northwest Company received from all posts in all departments 77,500 beaver skins; 51,033 muskrat; 40,440 marten; and only 1,135 buffalo robes.

It was not until in the eighteen-thirties that the shaggy bulk of the buffalo overshadowed the fur trade. In 1820 Daniel Harmon, in his deadly *Journal of Voyages,* wrote: "The animal is first mentioned, the skins of which will be the greatest in value—purchased and exported by the North West Company; and so on to the least: Beaver, Otter, Muskrat, Martin, Bear, Fox, Lynx, Fisher, Mink, Wolf, Buffaloe."

But it was as food for the partisans, the *voyageurs,* the *coureurs de bois,* the *mangeurs de lard,* the *hivernans,* the whole body of men that the great fur-trading organizations kept in the field, that the buffalo was vitally important to the fur trade.

From the more remote districts, Peace River, the Saskatchewan, Lake Athabasca, the most valuable furs were obtained. These distant posts had to take their living from the country about them; and the country supported them handsomely.[2] At Fort Ed-

[2] Pierre Jean de Smet, *Oregon Missions* (R. G. Thwaites, *Early Western Travels,* Vol. XXIX); Alexander Henry, *Travels and Adventures in Canada . . .* (New York, 1809). The author of the *Travels* is the "first" Alexander Henry, not to be confused with the "Nor'-wester."

See the neat sketch by Merriman, "The Bison and the Fur Trade,"

monton, the great emporium of the Hudson's Bay Company in the Upper Saskatchewan—Lake Athabasca district, Father de Smet found a permanent "family" of about eighty including the ladies of the forest and their children. "On my arrival at the Fort, the ice-house contained thirty thousand white fish, each weighing four pounds, and five hundred buffaloes, the ordinary amount of the winter provisions." For the weeks in the wilderness taken by trips to and from these posts, pemmican was the staple food.

In the eight years beginning in 1800, the Northwest Company used 21,250 pounds of pemmican and about ten tons of grease, dried meat, tongues, and humps from the Lower Red River Department for its canoemen and trappers elsewhere. The Hudson's Bay Company tapped the Red River valley also for great quantities of pemmican.

Then the plague came.

The Red River Settlement was the first invasion of plowmen into the buffalo plains of the north— alone in the great expanse of the fur traders' territory.

a *Bulletin* (1926) of Queens University, Kingston, Ontario. Incidentally, this is the most successful short monograph upon the American bison. Trexler, "The Buffalo Range of the Northwest," *Mississippi Valley Historical Review,* VII, and Mair, "The American Bison," *Transactions of the Royal Society of Canada,* VIII, should be mentioned.

Thomas Douglas, fifth Earl of Selkirk, was its founder. The Highland crofters, his countrymen, in the Anglicizing of Scotland had been evicted from their grain fields, and their little farms had been pieced together to make sheepwalks. Douglas wanted to bring these landless tenants back to the land; and when he became Earl of Selkirk he had the power.

He knew Alexander Mackenzie's book, *Voyages from Montreal and the River St. Lawrence,* much talked of in 1801 and 1802. Mackenzie was a partner in the Northwest Company, who had gone through the country of the Athabascan Indians and on into an Eskimo village and brought back reports of great abundance of buffaloes, moose, deer, beavers, wild fowl, about Great Slave Lake and the banks of the Peace River. Douglas himself toured Canada in 1803 and 1804. In May of 1804 he was in Montreal; and the Beaver Club honored him with a chair at its table. None belonged but the fur barons, the Nor'westers; they wore medals engraved "Fortitude in Distress," they chorused the boat-songs of the *voyageurs,* they banqueted on venison, bear steaks, and buffalo tongues.

Buying his way into the directorate of the Hudson's Bay Company, Douglas secured a grant ("for a consideration" of ten shillings) of 116,000 square miles south of the Narrows of Lake Winnipeg and including most of the valley of the Red River of the North.

The Selkirk colonists [3] were at the southern shore of Hudson's Bay by autumn of 1811; and in midsummer of the next year, in four boats of their own making they pushed their way up the Hayes River for the interior—rowing against the current, making a portage, and rowing again—about three hundred and thirty miles to the northernmost arm of Lake Winnipeg, and only one trading post in that distance. Soon the party was moving slowly down the low-lying eastern shore of Lake Winnipeg; and beyond the tall reeds at the lake's edge they first saw the great prairie. The last stage of the journey was down Red River, to the bend two miles below the confluence of the Red and the Assiniboine; and on the fourth of September six swivel cannons hailed the hoisting of the British ensign over the lonely little settlement.

The provisions brought from Hudson's Bay were already fast diminishing. John Winthrop's Puritan charges had faced just such destitution in their first winter in Massachusetts, and that colony had barely survived; but the Highlanders confronting their first winter on the Canadian plain had herds of

[3] Louis A. Wood, *The Red River Colony* (Toronto, 1920); George Bryce, *Romantic Settlement of Lord Selkirk's Colonists* (New York, 1912); various articles and addresses in *Publications of the State Historical Society of North Dakota*, Vol. II.

great game animals roaming within a few miles of them. There was ample, excellent food for these first settlers and for a second contingent that arrived in midwinter. Buffalo herds that in summer were near the banks of the Saskatchewan traveled in their winter migration to the plateau ribboned by the little Pembina River, which flows into Red River near the present boundary of Minnesota. Here the Indians guided the novice hunters; a storehouse and cabins were put up, a palisade was circled about the encampment, and until spring the colonists stayed at Pembina. The buffalo were so many and so near that occasionally they could be shot from the palisades.

In the next year, when the slush had disappeared, they found that the ground could not be broken up by light hoes, the only tilling implements they had; the berry bushes, for some reason, bore no fruit; and the river contained only a few small schools of fish. The colonists went again to Pembina; but in the winter of 1813-14 the plateau was swathed with heavy snowdrifts, and the buffaloes had been forced farther south by the unusual cold. Without the buffalo, the Highlanders had to stint themselves on the little food they could buy from the Indians.

New colonists and new implements invigorated Red River Settlement in the summer of 1814. And when the colony had found its strength the inevitable war with the fur traders began.

The Nor'westers knew that even this small settlement, once permanently planted in the buffalo range, would exterminate the buffalo herds that were accustomed to come within a hundred miles of the place, just as a handful of settlers had driven the buffalo from Kentucky. With the buffalo gone, and with the beaver streams in the vicinity despoiled, this region would gape, a barren circle, in the middle of the fur country.

The settlement forced the issue by proclaiming it unlawful for any person who dealt in furs to remove pemmican or other food supplies from Selkirk's lands; and when the Nor'westers made it plain that they intended to send pemmican from Selkirkia to their distant posts, as they had done for fourteen years, Governor Macdonnell of the settlement battered his way into the company's storehouse and seized six hundred bags of pemmican. Thus the Pemmican War began, and it continued, bloody and discreditable to both sides, until the war reached an anticlimax in the deliberations of Canadian courts. In 1818 the colonists were no longer fighting Nor'westers, but pestilent swarms of locusts.

The merging of the Northwest Company into the Hudson's Bay Company in the spring of 1821 left the Red River Settlement secure in its anchorage among the buffaloes. The colony plunged immediately into high speculation: the buffaloes were to make every one wealthy. The "Buffalo Wool Company" was established, sample squares of cloth made from the wool of the buffalo were distributed in London and aroused a fashionable curiosity; wages in the company skyrocketed, and the settlement was intoxicated with visions of grandeur. Ten thousand dollars were raised by the sale of stock, and the Hudson's Bay Company, as bankers for the Buffalo Wool Company, advanced twenty-two thousand and five hundred dollars more. In the next year the bubble burst. A yard of buffalo wool cost about twelve dollars and a half to manufacture; and, even priced as a novelty, could not bring more than a dollar and ten cents in London. The capital and the loan were swallowed up, and the chastened colony settled down to agriculture.

Many of the French-Canadian hunters—the Métis—who had been attached to Fort William, or to one of the sixty Nor'west trading posts which that great supply station served, asked to be given homes in Selkirkia. If Alexander Ross, the local historian of the colony's later years, remembered the address faithfully, the council gave the Métis a grandiose welcome: "My friends! in coming to Red River you evince a laudable feeling, a determination to throw off your savage customs, follow the habits of white men, and cultivate civilization. If these are your views, the Company will hold out the right hand of fellowship, and give you every encouragement; but remember, there is no field here for the pursuit of your savage life; you must settle down, cultivate the soil, and become Christians."

But against the tang of the buffalo hunt the good intentions of the half-breeds to become established, agrarian, and dull counted for nothing. Many of them drifted back into the fur trade, signing articles at the newly built Hudson's Bay post, Fort Garry; and those that remained on farms lived indolently on pemmican and jerked meat, and such crops as chose to grow without coaxing, until they set out for the hunt again.

By the first of June, "the hunters are in motion, like bees, and the whole colony in a state of confusion. It is now that the Company, the farmers . . . are all beset by their incessant and irresistible importunities. One wants a horse, another an ax, a third a cart; they want clothing, they want provisions; and though a whole people may refuse one or two they cannot deny a whole population, for indeed over much obstinacy would not be unattended with risk." [4] And when the hunters left the

[4] Alexander Ross, *The Red River Settlement* (London, 1856).

settlement, added Ross, the Scotchmen enjoyed that relief "which a person feels on recovering from a long and painful sickness."

When the hunters neared Pembina, the camp formed in a circle on the plain, and set about electing a president of the hunt, and captains and policemen. There were laws that every hunter had to observe. No buffalo were to be run on the Sabbath. No party could lag behind or fork off from the main body without permission. The greatest of offenses was for any one to run the buffalo, or discharge his gun, before a general order was given the whole camp. If any one violated the laws of this hunting republic, his saddle and bridle were cut to pieces.

On the morning of the buffalo chase, after the priest accompanying the expedition had said mass, the hunters were drawn up in line; cautiously they approached the herd; and with the president's roar "Ho!" the chase was on. "Imagine four hundred horsemen entering at full speed a herd of some thousands of buffalo, all in rapid motion," invited a spectator. "Riders in clouds of dust and volumes of smoke . . . crossing and recrossing each other in every direction; shots on the right, on the left, behind, before . . . two, three, a dozen at a time . . . horses stumbling, riders falling, dead and wounded animals tumbling here and there, one over the other." The zigzag mêlée went on for an hour or two; but a veteran of these hunts, when the fugitive buffaloes were out of range and the hunt was over, could recross the field and recognize every animal he had killed—and explain how he killed it.

On the hunt of 1840 over twelve hundred carts were driven to Pembina—two-wheeled, wooden things, the parts held doubtfully together by wooden pegs, and each cart in transit groaning to an original tune. Four hundred buffalo-running horses, and draught horses and oxen for the carts were taken along. Not less than twenty-five hundred buffaloes were killed; but out of that number only three hundred and seventy-five bags of pemmican and two hundred and forty bales of dried meat were made. Seven hundred and fifty buffaloes would have been ample for that result; but the great characteristic of all western hunts, of buffalo, elk, or antelope, was waste.

Returning to Red River Settlement, the expedition of 1840 brought over a million pounds of buffalo meat—about nine hundred pounds in a cart. As soon as the hunters arrived, the Hudson's Bay Company announced that it would buy pemmican, dried meat, and tallow at its established price of twopence a pound. From this sale of food to the fur traders the hunters got as much money, or more, as the staid Highlanders received for the produce of their season's work in the fields.

In the twenty years from the end of the Pemmican War to 1840, the hunters to the Red River Settlement (to keep track of the one great annual hunt and not to attempt an estimate of the kill of the small parties of half-breeds who hunted at Pembina in the winter) killed over six hundred and fifty thousand buffalo. The result was just what the Nor'westers had tried to fend off: the extermination of the buffalo from the Winnipeg prairie. Throughout the whole of Manitoba, and throughout northern Minnesota and northeastern Dakota, there were no herds of buffalo after 1847. Hunters who went westward from Red River Settlement to the Qu'Appelle and the Saskatchewan did their work of destruction almost as thoroughly.

The Crees of the Plains, whose country was around the headwaters of the Qu'Appelle, two hundred and fifty miles west of the Red River Settlement, in 1857 resolved in council that: "in consequence of the promises often made and broken by white men and half breeds, and the rapid destruction by them of the buffalo they fed on, they would not permit either white men or half-breeds to hunt in their territory, or travel through it, except for the purpose of trading for their dried meat, pemmican, skins, and robes." The Indian and the buffalo were making a last stand together. About the Hudson's Bay Company posts men were handling unfamiliar spades, and planting wheat; and they remembered that "pork-eater" once meant "tenderfoot."

CHAPTER V

LONG before American demand and American whiskey flung little groups of traders into the West to stud the Missouri and its tributaries with posts and *caches,* Indian tribes bartered with Indian tribes for buffalo robes and buffalo meat.

The Assiniboines as early as 1738 were trading with the Mandans, bringing muskets, axes, kettles, powder, bullets, knives, bodkins, which they secured from the British at Hudson's Bay, and taking from the Mandans—whose craft in working furs and feathers was beyond the ability of the northern tribe—painted buffalo robes, clusters of painted feathers, headdresses, garters, and girdles. The Snake Indians, found by Colonel Astor's overland traders in 1810 in a region deserted by buffalo, were clad in buffalo robes, for which they had traded salmon to the hunting tribes. The Bannock Indians traded with the Nez Perces for horses, giving in exchange buffalo robes, buffalo meat, and beaver. Before the planting of American trading posts, the Cayuse tribe was accustomed to hold a rendezvous at *La Grande Rounde,* a valley in the Blue Mountains, with the Shoshones and other tribes, and exchanging with them their horses for buffalo robes, tepees of buffalo skin, and varied craft work.

In the Red River valley of the South, the Panis Indians, reported Lieutenant Cutler in 1812, grew pumpkins, which they cut into strips for drying, and wove the wilted strips into mats; they traded this resilient chewing stuff to the Comanches. The Comanches were roving Indians, buffalo hunters; and they chewed the pumpkin mats, *pour passer le temps,* as they rode. The Panis took buffalo robes and horses in payment.

When the great American fur companies—Lisa's Missouri Fur Company, Astor's American Fur Company, Ashley's Rocky Mountain Company— began their exploitation of the West, they found the Indians ready enough to trade for buffalo robes. Except for the Blackfeet, no tribe was consistently hostile to the fur traders. What an early traveler said of the Cheyennes—"They do not cultivate, but bring to market buffaloe robes of the best quality, and are well disposed toward the whites"—was fairly true of the other nomadic tribes. The gathering of buffalo robes was an extensive occupation of the Pawnees; fur traders were regularly sent out from Council Bluffs to live with the Pawnees

A CHASE

From George Catlin, *North American Indian Portfolio* (George Catlin, London, n. d.).

at their lodges and follow them on their hunting forays. The Sioux, the largest and most important group with whom the traders had traffic, incessantly hunted the buffalo, and brought great quantities of robes to the many trading posts within the Sioux country.

But in the golden age of the fur trade beaver was the most important peltry, and the tedious work of baiting, setting, and collecting traps was another matter. The Omahas and Sioux were good beaver traders; the Assiniboines, Aricaras, and other tribes were little disposed to such work. As Alexander Ross described the Blackfeet: "Their occupations were war and buffalo hunting. Their country did not abound in furs, nor would men accustomed to an indolent and roving life submit to the drudgery of killing beavers. They spurned the idea of crawling about the country in search of furs; 'Such a life,' they said, 'was only fit for women and slaves.'" And in default of a steady supply of beaver from the Indians, the trading companies brought their own trappers—*voyageurs* who had drifted down from Canada, Frenchmen from the Louisiana settlements, American frontiersmen— into the Indian country.

Some of these trappers remained attached to company trading posts; some, the "lone trappers," attained a remarkable independence. The winter camp of a lone trapper was a dugout or a shanty, in a spot screened by rocks or bushes; beside it were his frames for stretching the skins, and facing the shanty a pole lifted upon crotches and supporting an array of the ribs, shoulders, choice cuts, of buffalo and deer. "Thus conditioned are these lordly rangers in their mountain home, nor own that any creature of human kind can possibly enjoy life better than they." The lone trapper made his clothes from the skins of his kill; even his shoes were made of buffalo hide, or deer skin. The easy acquisition of a squaw or two from the tribe of his vicinity gave him free license to trap and hunt in that tribe's range: "A horse, a flint gun, some white cloth and beads, could purchase the heart and hand of the fairest squaw in Prairie land. If she did not love after one of these valuable 'presents' had been made to her father, the lodge-poles were always handy to enforce that obedience necessary to domestic happiness." [1]

General Ashley, the moving spirit of the Rocky Mountain Fur Company, introduced the institution of the summer rendezvous. To these gatherings, in a certain valley or about a landmark, came the company's traders with their packs, and Indians and

[1] For the life of the Indian trader, see Alexander Ross, *Adventures of the First Settlers* (R. G. Thwaites, *Early Western Travels,* Vol. VII); R. B. Sage, *Scenes in the Rocky Mountains* (Philadelphia, 1846); and W. F. Butler, *The Wild North Land* (Philadelphia, 1874).

free trappers with an additional wealth of furs. The German physician-traveler, Wislizenus, saw the last of these rendezvous, in 1839: "The Indians had for trade chiefly tanned skins, moccasins, thongs of buffalo leather or braided buffalo hair, and fresh or dried buffalo meat. They have no beaver skins. The articles that attracted them most in exchange were powder and lead, knives, tobacco, cinnabar, gaily colored kerchiefs, pocket mirrors and all sorts of ornaments. . . . The peltry bought from the Indians must be carefully beaten and aired, at peril of having objectionable troops billeted on you. The Indians, accustomed to every kind of uncleanliness, seem to have a special predilection for a certain kind of domestic animal, and even to consider it a delicacy." [2]

In the many trading posts—some of them elaborate and strong, almost fortresses, like Fort Laramie, and some like Fort Bridger ("It is built of poles and daubed with mud; it is a shabby concern")—buffalo meat was the common staple. The larger posts had hunters whose sole duty was to keep the supply of *dépouille,* tongue, ribs, apace with the demands of the habitants and their voracious squaws. In 1805 Daniel Harmon estimated that the "family" of seventy persons at Fort Alex-

[2] F. A. Wislizenus, *A Journey to the Rocky Mountains in 1839* (St. Louis, 1912).

[89]

andria, in the Swan River region, consumed four hundred and fifty pounds of buffalo meat daily; in view of the recorded allowance at certain Hudson's Bay posts of eight pounds of buffalo meat as one man's daily ration, the group at Fort Alexandria must have consumed eight tons of buffalo for each month of the winter.

Kenneth McKenzie, the ablest trader ever in the service of the American Fur Company, had been in command of its upper Missouri outfit only a year when he built Fort Union, in the fall of 1828. This fort, at the mouth of the Yellowstone, united the fur-trade routes of the rivers and of the mountains —the best-built and best-equipped post west of the Mississippi. The steamboat *Yellowstone* was another creation of his vigorous imagination. By midsummer of 1830 McKenzie had convinced his superiors in the company that a small steamboat, such as could be built for seven or eight thousand dollars, could ascend the Missouri as far as the mouth of the Yellowstone, and return to St. Louis by the first of July laden with the season's catch of furs— and this without the delays, the losses, and the expense of men incident upon keel boats and bull boats.

In the spring and summer of 1832 the boat made its first voyage to Fort Union. Pierre Chouteau, Jr., fur trader, and George Catlin, artist, were distinguished passengers. After fighting past the snags and sandbars of the lower part of the river, the *Yellowstone* entered a green country, hilled and ravined, where astonished herds of buffalo, of antelopes, elk, wolves, coyotes, mountain goats, bounded away from the sight and the noise of the steamboat. Indians left their villages to look at the "big thunder canoe," that saw its own way, and followed the deep water of the channel; and when an audience was at the river bank the captain ordered the discharge of cannon, or opened the steam-exhaust valve to lend a horrisonant majesty to the great business of fur trading.

Fort Union, the destination, was built on an alluvial rise between the Missouri and the Yellowstone. About the fort was a palisade of foot-thick pickets about twenty feet high; the two bastions, at the southwest and northeast corners, were entirely of stone. Within the square were the residences of McKenzie, the clerks, the interpreters, and the *engagés,* the powder magazines, storerooms, stables, workshops, and rooms for receiving the Indians; in the center of the square was the flagstaff, and beside it a cannon with its mouth pointing toward the entrance gate.[3].

[3] Descriptions of life at Fort Union are incorporated in Prince Maximilian, *Travels in the Interior of North America* (Thwaites, *op. cit.,* Vol. XXII) and in George Catlin, *North American Indians* (latest

McKenzie (Catlin called him "a kind-hearted and high-minded Scotchman") was a gastronome, who kept his spacious ice box stocked with buffalo tongues, marrow fat and *dépouille,* and beaver tails, bears' feet, and the other delicacies of the game country. Port and madeira were his most precious importations, and a bottle of each perfumed every dinner; American-like, he always iced his wines.

When there was need of replenishing the meats, McKenzie himself led the hunt, conscious that he was the most distinguished buffalo hunter among the white men of the region. First he called four or five of his men, and told them to follow his trail with carts: "You will find us on the plain yonder, between the Yellowstone and the Missouri rivers, with meat enough to load you home."

Then the hunting party crossed the river, and mounted the bluff; and in full view—on that occasion when George Catlin had his first buffalo hunt—was a herd of four or five hundred buffaloes, some grazing, some lying down. One of the hunters "tossed the feather," an invariable custom, to determine the course of the wind; then hats and coats were taken off, sleeves rolled up, and, the preliminaries fixed, the party mounted and approached the herd. The approach was slow and quiet, to get

edition Edinburgh, 1926), Vol. I. See also Hiram M. Chittenden, *The American Fur Trade of the Far West* (3 vols.: New York, 1902).

the party as near the resting buffalo as possible before the herd took alarm. The horses were fully in
the spirit of the chase: "the laziest nag amongst
them prances with an elasticity in his step—champ-
ing his bit—his ears erect—his eyes strained
out of his head, and fixed on the game before
him, while he trembles under the saddle of his
rider."

The instant the herd discovered its danger and
wheeled about, the horses, who needed no cue,
stretched out after them. In a cloud of dust they
reached the buffalo. McKenzie was foremost, and
dashed off into the dust after the fattest of the fleet
cows. Catlin rode "scarcely able to tell whether I
was on a buffalo's back or my horse—hit, and
hooked, and jostled about, till at length I found myself alongside my game, when I gave him a shot, as
I passed him. I saw guns flash in several directions
about me, but I heard them not."

When the herd, the pursuers, and the dust had
passed, Catlin went back to his wounded bull. The
bull had regained his feet; but one leg was useless.
He bristled with fury; made a mad lunge; and fell
on his nose. Catlin was fascinated with the picture
of awful anger: "I defy the world to produce another animal that can look as frightful as a huge
buffalo bull, when wounded as he was, turned
around for battle, and swelling with rage—his eyes

bloodshot, and his long shaggy mane hanging to the ground—his mouth open, and his horrid rage hissing in streams of smoke and blood."

When the party had regathered, pipes were lit, and each man accounted for his own killings. The old hunters were amused at Catlin's choice—an old bull, too tough and stringy for eating. Catlin rode back beside McKenzie, who pointed out the five fat, slick cows he had killed—one bullet for each cow, straight through the heart every time. That was McKenzie for you!

North of McKenzie's fort were the Assiniboines; west were the Crees and the Blackfeet; south were the Crow Indians. The Mandans had their villages about the Missouri River to the east. The Crows were great buffalo hunters, and the fur companies regarded them as the best robe producers of any of the Indian tribes; but they put the fur traders to no little trouble to satisfy their whims. The method finally adopted was to keep traders with small outfits of goods permanently in their villages, moving when the Indians moved. The Assiniboines and the Blackfeet were good robe makers, but no tribe was as adept at dressing the robes as the Crows. The chief staples which the Mandans offered were the robes and the tongues of the buffalo. These relations with the buffalo-hunting tribes of the upper Missouri gave the American Fur Company a great advantage in the new era of the fur trade, which had just begun.

.   .   .   .

In the early eighteen-thirties, when the fashion in dresses was running to flounces, scallops, flutings, sleeves *en gigot* and rich lacings, the mode for gentlemen was also changing—to the supremacy of the silk topper, and the doom of the beaver hat. John Jacob Astor early forecast the end of the beaver trade. *Silliman's Journal* made the prediction more sweeping, in 1834: "It appears that the fur trade must henceforth decline. The advanced state of geographical knowledge shows that no countries remain to be explored. In North America the animals are slowly decreasing, from the persevering efforts and the indiscriminate slaughter practiced by hunters, and by the appropriation to the use of man of those rivers and forests which have afforded them food and protection. They recede with the aborigines, before the tide of civilization." Astor, old and wealthy, decided to recede with the beaver, and sold his American Fur Company—the Northern Department, and with it the right to the old name, to Ramsay Crooks and his associates, and the Western Department, with its headquarters at St. Louis, to Pratte, Chouteau and Company.

With the veer in fashion buffalo robes came into new prominence. In the business of Chouteau and

Crooks buffalo robes exceeded in bulk all other furs combined, and in value occasionally led the field, occasionally lagged behind the value of beaver. The old type trapper, the lone dweller, became less and less in evidence, and the business of trading rested upon agents among the Indians, and upon buffalo hunters who lived in company forts, or threw in their fortunes—whole hog or none: squaw, war parties, and stewed dog—with the Indians. On his second exploring expedition Colonel Fremont, leaving the valley of the South Platte, could not secure a guide: "It is singular that, immediately at the foot of the mountains, I could find no one sufficiently acquainted with them to guide me to the plains at their western base; but the race of trappers who formerly lived in their recesses has almost entirely disappeared—dwindled to a few scattered individuals."

Pierre Chouteau at St. Louis and the American Fur Company kept always in close association. Ramsay Crooks, writing to Chouteau in the spring of 1835, notes that "the short crop of buffalo robes disappointed many dealers last year, and we have orders already for the whole of the next collection if it be 36,000 or even more." And the two agree to dispose of summer skins—skins taken when the buffalo fur was thinnest and poorest, and consequently of little value—by packing their robes in packs of twelve, eleven seasonable robes and one summer skin. The company was to sell the pack at forty-eight dollars; to fix a price of two dollars and a half for a calf skin, and to price other skins proportionately. The company might obtain a higher price, Crooks pointed out, but in that case a few large retailers would buy the entire collection, and doubtless carry over a large stock of robes that would embarrass the company the season after. It seemed more prudent to make the rates "moderate" and divide the robes "among so many hands as will create a competition and restrain them from putting too high a value on the article, thereby insuring the consumption of the whole collection annually, and leaving the market clear for the succeeding crop."

The President of the American Fur Company urged that the robes sent down the Mississippi to New Orleans and thence cargoed to New York be hurried in and out of New Orleans warehouses as quickly as possible, saving them from the vermin active in so hot a climate; and, further, that "they should always in shipping them see that they are stowed *between decks* and not in the *lower* hold, and if this can be done, it is well worth paying something for it, as in the *lower* hold your packs are liable to come into contact with Hides, Sheepskins, and other pernicious neighbours, who never fail to do considerable injury to both Deerskins and Buffalo Robes." [4]

But in the summer of 1835 the steamboat *Assiniboine,* whose cargo included many packs of Chouteau's buffalo robes, was destroyed, and the cargo lost. By the President's recommendation the price on robe packs was raised to about sixty dollars, to meet the reduction in quantity.

Robes were sometimes sent from St. Louis by way of Pittsburgh; but those that came overland usually arrived in New York very tardily, and more or less damaged.

In 1837 Pratte, Chouteau and Company fairly glutted the market with buffalo robes. A surplus of 23,000 robes was carried over into the season of 1838. Crooks estimated that the trading of 1838 would bring over 51,000 new robes into market; and that with 9,500 robes remaining in the hands of rival fur companies, 84,700 robes would have to be disposed of in the coming season. He attempted to make Chouteau agree that "you shall not send East of the Allegheny more than 30,000 skins of this

[4] MS. Papers of the American Fur Company, in possession of the New York Historical Society. In the following few pages sentences are quoted from the following letters: Crooks to Chouteau, March 7, 1835, August 1, 1838, August 15, 1840, February 12, 1840; Known (of Albany) to Crooks, November 12, 1840; Crooks to Chouteau, July 21, 1838; Klancke (of Hamburg) to Crooks, March 25, 1842, May 3, 1842; Crooks to Klancke, August 31, 1842; and Klancke to Crooks, January 26, 1844. And, of course, see Chittenden, *op. cit.*

year's collection, nor sell to anyone for exports to this quarter, but you may sell for the consumption of any part of the western country no nearer than Pittsburgh," and that Chouteau's 30,000 robes were to be divided solely among the "friends" of the American Fur Company.

But the western traffic in buffalo robes was insatiate. Slaughter continued to outdistance the demand. Crooks wrote to Chouteau in mid-August, 1840: "We take to note all of your shipments of buffalo robes and shall do the best we can for your interest, and though you keep back all the bad, the quantity remaining unsold of the crop of 1839, those in the hand of this year's collection, what you will probably ship to the market will make an aggregate we fear beyond the demand, even if the demand proves ever so favorable." And Chouteau promptly proceeded to capsize the market with shipments that autumn of 67,000 buffalo robes.

The mode would not be satisfied with second-grade robes or mended robes. Customers endlessly complained. In February of 1840 Ramsay Crooks addressed Chouteau: "Each man who bought a pack this season does not only grumble but insists on allowances that would swallow up your profits and some of the capital. We shall do all we fairly can to diminish these claims for damage; but if we are compelled to make some deduction for inferiority of quality, it will apply to almost every robe you sent us this season."

In the summer of 1840 Pierre Chouteau ordered for his winter bartering with the Indians, for buffalo robes and other furs, six thousand pairs of French blankets; three hundred "North West English guns," which cost him $5.62½ each; three hundred dozen butcher knives; nine thousand pounds of blue and white chalk beads; five hundred pounds of "Pigeon Egg Beads"; and a quantity of cloth goods from English manufacturers.

An Indian agent once roundly denounced the methods of the American Fur Company in the West: "They have enslaved the Indians; kept them in ignorance; taken from them year after year their pitiful earnings . . ." The conduct of business in the East did not strongly contradict the company's unofficial title of "most corrupt institution." The company's files are thickened with complaints of misrepresentations—from the matter-of-record protests of disillusioned old buyers to the puzzled queries of new customers: "The last parcel of Upper Missouri skins we had from you were very inferior, the Bales weighing from ten to twelve pounds lighter than the Sioux skins which cost twenty-five cents less. We have thought there must be some mistake in sending them . . ."

The company had no strong competitors in the

buffalo-robe trade, but it kept the watch of a hawk over the weakest sort of rivalry. Crooks, writing to Chouteau about the competition of Powell, Lamont and Company, who had a few thousand robes in the autumn of 1838, advises his associate: "If you desire to keep up the prices, it will be bad policy to go into competition with these 5,000 skins. The sooner they are out of the way the better, and if we can buy them we had better do so—there is no danger of his getting a large price for them in Boston, but whatever success he may have, it seems to me like madness to allow his small quantity to influence the value of your large one. We cannot possibly think of putting the price of your Buffaloes so low that Mr. Powell will prefer keeping his, to letting them go at our rate, or in proportion to it. He must sell, we presume, and while it will be our aim to prevent his getting rich by the transaction, we see no way of getting off ours and preventing the sale of his. We shall look after his movements and take all possible care of your interest in the matter."

In the early forties, Ramsay Crooks made an ambitious attempt to create a market for buffalo robes in Europe. Ten packs of robes were sent to a furrier in Hamburg in the winter of 1841-42. The agent gave wide publicity to their arrival, and to the uses and qualities of buffalo robes, but only a limited number of dealers—"mostly attracted by curiosity"

—appeared at the auction, and the highest bid was below the cost of the robes.

Klancke, the agent in Hamburg, sent a sample bale of five buffalo robes to Leipzig, the chief market for Russian and Polish furriers; but here he found, as in Hamburg, that buffalo robes would be preferred generally for the use of military service covers, coats for travel wear, sledge covers, and carriage carpets—if it were not for the price. Imported buffalo could not compete with native sheepskin. Crooks wrote Klancke that his St. Louis associates were "pretty well satisfied that unless our skins are preferred for some particular use that will induce buyers to pay a much higher price than for your five sheep skins, we may despair of success. Would they not find a good market in Russia, for their sleighs, in place of the Bear-skins so generally used, and which must be more expensive than our buffaloes?"

But the agent in Hamburg was discouraged, and lamented: "My good countrymen are rather heavy and stubborn in point of new customs and nuances, mechanically adhering to the old without being of a speculative cast or turn." When in the winter of 1843-44 the prices of buffalo robes declined, Klancke found a market, but a limited one. In London the trade in buffalo robes was much better.

In 1843 an official of the American Fur Company

gave Fremont the information: "The total amount of robes annually traded by ourselves and others will not be found to differ much from the following statement:

American Fur Company..... 70,000 robes,
Hudson's Bay Company..... 10,000 robes,
All other companies, probably 10,000 robes,

. . . as an average annual return for the last eight or ten years." Besides the robe trade, there was extensive trade in tongues and in tallow. In 1848 the number of buffalo tongues sent to St. Louis reached 25,000; and the number of buffalo robes reached 100,000. Were the great herds dwindling? As soon talk of a shortage of whiskey or pigeon-egg beads.

CHAPTER VI

WESTWARD THE COURSE

"IT IS a matter of considerable importance to prevent the encroachment of our citizens on lands belonging to the Indians of our South Western frontier," wrote John C. Calhoun, then Secretary of War, to the commandant of the Natchitoches post, "and to prevent our people from passing into the Buffalo Country, either for the destruction of game or to traffick with the Indians without license." Within the boundaries of the States the Indians, surly farmers, could have no permanent home: there was no trusting them to keep the peace, there was no land they might occupy into which white farmers and backwoodsmen would not filter. But beyond the Missouri lay the Great Plains, ill-watered and unfit for farming (Calhoun's generation was sure); but abundant with game, occupied only by Indians, whose numbers—say, two hundred and twenty-five thousand—were a very light tax on the great herds of buffalo, the herds of deer and antelope, and the smaller game. In 1832 the Indian country became a legal entity, and by Act of Congress no white person without license from the Indian Commissioner was to set foot within this permanent home of the American Indian. None of the gentlemen in authority had the wild fancy that within another generation the Great Plains would be transversed by squirming, many-rutted roadways—for freighters and bullwhackers to Santa Fe, schooners and emigrant settlers to the South Pass, miners to California, Mormons to Salt Lake. A few men in Missouri must have guessed at the magnitude of the coming wave.

Thomas Jefferson made the first move to cleave a highway of exploration through the West, while the far reaches of that West were still in alien hands. Three months and a half before the French and American representatives in Paris had agreed upon the Louisiana Purchase, the President had advised Congress: "An intelligent officer, with ten or twelve chosen men, fit for the enterprise and willing to undertake it, taken from our posts where they may be spared without inconvenience, might explore the whole line, even to the Western Ocean, have conferences with the natives on the subject of commercial intercourse, get admission among them for our traders as others are admitted, agree on convenient deposits for an interchange of articles, and return with the information required in the course of two summers." And on the twentieth of

June, 1803, Meriwether Lewis was formally advised that he should conduct an expedition from the mouth of the Missouri to the western shore of the continent.

The voyage up the Missouri began in the middle of May, 1804. On the sixth of June William Clark wrote in his *Journal:* "Some buffalow Sign today." That is the first direct mention of buffalo in the journals of the expedition. Jefferson had advised Lewis to make detailed mention of the wild animals of the West; and there is reference after reference to buffalo herds seen on the prairie, to Indian hunts after buffalo, to buffalo killed and eaten by the expedition. Up the Missouri, just leaving the mouth of the Vermillion, on August the twenty-fifth, writes Clark, "we beheld a most butifull landscape; Numerous herds of buffalow were seen feeding in various directions." This was the beginning. On the twenty-first of the next month the party reached "a butifull inclined Plain, in which there is great numbers of Buffalow, Elk & Goats in view feeding & scipping on those Plains Grouse, Larks & the Prairie bird is Common in those Plains." And thirty days later, in Clark's handwriting, "I observe near all large Gangues of Buffalow wolves and when the buffalow move these animals follow, and feed on those that are killed by accident or those that are too pore or fat to keep up with the gangue." Herds

WHITE WOLVES ATTACKING A BUFFALO BULL

From George Catlin, *North American Indian Portfolio* (George Catlin, London, n. d.).

had now become too frequent to be mentioned, except when some vista of a buffalo-covered prairie strikes a burst of admiration that bubbles its way into the *Journal*.

When, after a winter among the Mandans, the party pushed on to the West, buffalo were frequently met until the mouth of the Musselshell was passed, when herds became scarce. At times the buffalo had fairly been a necessity to the travelers, and again a delight. At the Great Falls Portage on the Missouri, Lewis wrote: "Some hunters were sent out to kill buffaloe in order to make pemecon to take with us and also for their skins which we now want to cover our baggage in the boat and canoes when we depart from hence. the Indians have informed us that we should shortly leave the buffaloe country after passing the falls; this I much regret for I know when we leave the buffaloe that we shall sometimes be under the necessity of fasting occasionally, and at all events the white puddings will be irretrievably lost and Sharbono out of employment."

On the return journey in the summer of 1806, Sergeant Pryor, entrusted with returning the horses the travelers had obtained from the Mandans, could not keep the "cavvayard" together when the Indian ponies saw buffalo; "the loose horses, having been trained by the Indians to hunt, immediately set off in pursuit of them, and surrounded the buffalo herd with almost as much skill as their riders could have done. At last he was obliged to send one horseman forward and drive all the buffaloe from the route." On the twenty-ninth of August Clark "ascended to the high Country and from an eminance I had a view . . . of a greater number of buffalow than I had ever seen before at one time. I must have seen near 20,000 of those animals feeding on the plain."

After the great adventure of Lewis and Clark, fur traders—Smith, Colter, Walker, Pattie, Carson, Bridger, and many others—pushed up the streams, followed the watersheds, roamed the plains and the deserts of the West, and learned the ways of the Indian and the buffalo. Josiah Gregg, who wrote his history of the Santa Fe trade while Texas was yet a republic, said of the animals of the West: "they constitute so considerable a portion of the society of the traveller who journeys among them, that they get to hold somewhat the same place in his estimation that his fellow-creatures would occupy if he were in civilization. Indeed, the animals are *par eminence* the communities of the Prairies. By far the most noble of these . . . is the *mustang* or wild horse of the Prairies." With horse lovers, as with dog owners, there is no profit in arguing. "The *buffalo*," Gregg continues, "though making

[108]

no pretensions to the elegance and symmetry of the mustang, is by far the most important animal of the Prairies to the traveller." With these fur traders the buffalo was food and money. Later, with the travelers who kept notebooks and the emigrants who kept journals of the overland march, the buffalo was of living importance as a splendid object to see and to describe, and—again—as food.

Washington Irving wrote of Captain Bonneville's most pleasant encounter with the Bannock Indians: "Some men are said to wax valorous on a full stomach, and such seemed to be the case with the Bannock braves, who, in proportion as they crammed themselves with buffalo meat, grew stout of heart until, the supper at an end, they began to chant war songs, setting forth their mighty deeds and the victories they had gained over the Blackfeet"— these victories, incidentally, being mostly fictitious. Bonneville's keg of alcohol and honey, fifty-fifty, seems to have had no happier effect upon Indian manners than a supper of buffalo meat, about ten pounds to each Indian. And Doctor Wislizenus adds in behalf of white men: "People who formerly were accustomed to eat scarcely a pound of meat daily, can consume eight and ten times as much of fresh buffalo meat."

A dinner served to eleven people about a camp fire, of an evening in the spring of 1820, consisted of the roasted loin of a buffalo; boiled buffalo meat; two boiled buffalo tongues; "the spinous processes" of the buffalo "roasted in the manner of spare-ribs"; sausages made of the minced tenderloin and fat of the buffalo; and a buffalo hump, roasted whole. This was a luxurious variety of dishes, intended especially to delight the two ladies in the party, the first white women to ascend the Missouri into the Indian country. "It is true that we have no vegetables whatever, but . . . we scarcely regret their absence." The buffalo hump, volunteers Edwin James in the contentment of his spirit, "was last evening placed in a hole dug in the earth for its reception, which had been previously heated by means of a strong fire in and upon it. It was now covered with cinders and earth, to the depth of about one foot, and a strong fire was made over it. In this situation it remained until it was taken up for the table today."

Buffalo tongues were most celebrated for food, and thousands of animals were killed for this delicacy alone. They were usually roasted on the spit. Travelers who had leisure and good advice learned that buffalo marrow was one of the sweetest treasures in the whole catalogue of esculents. "Oh, shade of Eude, the marrow-bones!" exclaims Grantley Berkeley, an English traveler, and the whole tradition of British reserve goes toppling before the roasted thigh bone of the buffalo. "The bone was brought to table in its full length, and they had some way of hitting it with the back of an axe which opened one side only, like the lid of a box. The bone then, when this lid was removed, exposed in its entire length a regular white roll of unbroken marrow, beautifully done. When hot, as the lid had kept it, and put on thin toast, it was perfection! On inquiry I found that the two extreme ends of the marrow-bone only were placed in the red embers, and the heat of the bone itself dressed the marrow." [1]

The first of the western highways was the Missouri River, linking the villages of the robe-collecting Indians of the northern range with the capital of the fur trade, St. Louis. Each spring, after the robes and furs of the winter's trading had accumulated in the fur company posts, the packs were brought down the river in keel boats, flatboats, and in bull boats. This last-named craft was a primitive float which the fur traders adopted from the Indians. They were convenient, made without much trouble, and overland travelers often made them, when a river must be crossed, to serve to keep their goods dry in the crossing. As Captain Boone showed

[1] G. F. Berkeley, *The English Sportsman in the Western Prairies* (London, 1861), p. 263; F. A. Wislizenus, *Journey to the Rocky Mountains*, p. 51; Edwin James, *Account of an Expedition* (R. G. Thwaites, *Early Western Travels*, Vol. XIV), p. 280.

his dragoonsmen how to construct them: "Get poles a little larger than a man's wrist and split them and bend them over . . . for the ribs of the boat, making the boat 8 or 10 feet long according to the size of the skin, and four or five, or six feet wider . . . Lay the skin (of the buffalo) down with the hair next the ribs and stretch it down to the whaling or rib which forms the gunwale of the boat, trim off the edges and cut loop holes through it and lash it along. . . . One of these boats is not easily paddled in a rapid current or in high wind. The safest way is for a man to wade or swim and tow the boat along. One of these boats will carry 800 lbs. To lash several together, they are placed two and two along side, and one in bow and stern, with poles lashed across the top." [2]

When steamboats were introduced on the Missouri, the passenger list was at first made up almost entirely of men connected with the fur trade. The bill of fare provided by the steamboat's stores was not pretentious: salt pork, hominy or cornmeal, and navy beans. But each steamboat employed hunters, whose work was to leave the boat about midnight (three or four hours before the boat regularly started), and scour the banks for game, keeping well ahead of the boat. Whenever game was killed

[2] Louis Pelzer, *Marches of the Dragoons in the Mississippi Valley* (Iowa City, 1917), p. 212.

INDIAN WOMAN DRESSING A BUFFALO SKIN

From Mrs. Mary H. Eastman, *The American Aboriginal Portfolio* (Lippincott, Grambo & Company, Philadelphia, 1853).

it was lugged to the bank, and picked up by the steamboat's yawl when the boat came up.

In spring the carcasses of buffalo in the upper Missouri, lodged on sandbars and islands or against the shores, were so many that passengers found the air almost intolerable.[3]

The Santa Fe Trail was the earliest of the great overland travel ways. Discounting the isolated expeditions of pioneer traders, unsuccessful because of the hostility of the Spanish officials of Taos and Santa Fe, the "commerce of the prairies" was opened in 1821, when the combined parties of Hugh Glenn, Indian trader, and Jacob Fowler, sportsman, traveled from the Arkansas River to the mountains of New Mexico. No provisions but salt were carried; the buffalo, and farther westward the antelope, offered ample food along the march. The successful revolt of Mexico brought with it the end of Spanish exclusiveness; and within five more years commissioners of the American Government were surveying a road to Santa Fe.

From Franklin or Independence, Missouri, the successive outfitting points of the trade, wagons lagged to Council Grove, a hundred and fifty miles away; and here at the forest grove about the waters of the Neosho, the caravans were organized, with

---

[3] H. M. Chittenden, *History of Early Steamboat Navigation on the Missouri River* (New York, 1903), Vol. I, pp. 125, 148.

officers, guards, even a chaplain. Thence the route was across the hard, parched Cimmaron desert; and then through the foothills of the Rockies to Santa Fe. Domestic cottons, hardware, a variety of manufactures, and fabrics were taken southwest; specie and buffalo robes were brought back.

Indians, hovering about the route of the Santa Fe traders, occasionally created a shortage of buffalo by driving the herds far back from the route, and turned a fair bit of business by selling dried meat to the travelers. If a traveler was not too hungry, he would notice that the squaws of the Kansas tribe "jerked" buffalo meat with sublime indifference to filth, and would prefer to turn aside and take chances of finding his own buffalo. The Pawnee and Osage Indians in 1825 undertook not to molest the caravans, in consideration of presents and merchandise offered them by Federal commissioners; but the Comanches were never disposed to share any part of their buffalo range with the whites.

The Oregon Trail, in the years just before 1840, had become a well-defined highway, had become an American idea as well as a road. That idea was colonization of the agricultural lands of the continent, wherever they might be: and it meant the end of the hunting range. But in the decade of the eighteen-forties the West of the Indian and the buffalo was an unconquerable wild, dangerous, long to cross, but at least offering an abundance of game to sustain the journey to the South Pass, the gateway to the Far West. The subjugation and decline of the Indian was freely predicted, for they were thieves and sometimes waylaid and killed small parties of travelers: the United States Government was going to protect its own citizens, if the Army had to kill every Indian in the West. But as to these stupid, easily frightened beasts, these buffalo in great herds on either side of the trail: what were the predictions of Josiah Gregg, and two or three army officers who had been many years on the Plains, worth against the overwhelming evidence of fact—the millions of buffalo roaming the plains? A caravan bound for Oregon encountered herd after herd of buffalo; instances were known of caravans detained for several days by immense herds grazing in its path that would 'not be turned out. An emigrant wrote of the buffalo:

"They were as thick as sheep ever seen in a field, and moved not until the caravan was within ten feet of them. They would then rise and flee at random, greatly affrighted, and snorting and bellowing to the equal alarm of the horses and mules." [4]

"Such is the excitement that generally prevails

[4] Obadiah Oakley, *Expedition to Oregon* (New York, 1914), pp. 9-10.

at the sight of these fat denizens of the prairies," as Josiah Gregg wrote, "that very few hunters appear able to refrain from shooting as long as the game remains within reach of their rifles; nor can they ever permit a fair shot to escape them." But emigrants had to learn that horses accustomed to grain were much weakened by feeding on grass alone, as the caravan crept over the prairie; and hot chases after buffalo cost the lives of many fine horses. The sight of the first band of buffalo excited the whole caravan: "Our few horses, about a dozen, were in great demand, and several went on foot. We dashed over the hills, and beheld with a thrill of pleasure, the first stragglers of these much-talked-of animals; pell-mell we charged the huge monsters, and poured in a brisk fire, which sounded like an opening battle; our horses were wild with excitement and fright; the balls flew at random—the flying animals, frantic with pain and rage, seemed imbued with many lives. One was brought to bay by whole volleys of shots; his eyeballs glared; he bore his tufted tail aloft like a black flag; then shaking his vast and shaggy mane in impotent defiance, he sank majestically to the earth, under twenty bleeding wounds." The emigrants of many a caravan could tell such a yarn. "Of all hunting in the world this is probably the most exciting," a Santa Fe trader declared. And General Custer shared this enthusiasm: "Repeatedly could I have placed the muzzle of my revolver against the shaggy body of the huge beast," he describes a chase, "yet each time would I withdraw the weapon, as if to prolong the excitement of the race. Mile after mile was traversed in this way." [5]

In the summer of 1849, after the Oregon Trail— up the North Fork of the Platte to Fort Laramie, around the Black Mountains to the South Pass— had been the route of caravans for over fifteen years, Captain Howard Stansbury was ordered to conduct an exploration and survey of the Salt Lake basin. In the valley of the Little Blue, eighteen days' march from Fort Leavenworth, he rested—the day was Sunday—and gave his men and the emigrants accompanying him an opportunity to hunt. They had killed no game in the eighteen days; there had been nothing left to kill along this well-traveled route. And on this Sunday's hunt, the whole party brought in only a duck, a muskrat, a snapping turtle, and one miserable antelope. The party was hungry for fresh meat, after days of salt meat without vegetables; the arrival of the antelope, poor as it was, was hailed by Stansbury's men with lively satisfac-

[5] G. A. Custer, *My Life on the Plains* (New York, 1874); G. W. Kendall, *Narrative of the Santa Fe Expedition* (New York, 1844); P. St. G. Cooke, *Scenes and Adventures in the Army* (London, 1859); W. H. Emory, "Notes of a Military Reconnaisance," Thirtieth Congress, First Session, Senate Document No. 7.

tion, and the little carcass was divided between half a dozen messes.

On the next day Stansbury left the Blue and crossed over into the valley of the Platte—a valley of two miles in breadth, rich green grass unrelieved by any shrub, a level floor to the muddy-white Platte. As Stansbury, on the ridge between the two rivers, looked over the green expanse, his guide commented that the last time he had passed this way the whole of the plain, as far as the eye could see, was black with herds of buffalo. Now, not one buffalo was to be seen; they had fled before the advancing tide of emigration.

Twenty-six days later, when the expedition was well up the valley of the Platte, Stansbury's hunters killed their first buffalo; but in order to obtain it, they had to ride four or five miles from the road, and go beyond the bluffs of the valley. "The eyes of our French *voyageurs* fairly glistened as they rode into camp laden with the meat, and their arrival was hailed with a general shout of congratulation. The long-desired spoil was soon divided, and a long scene ensued of roasting, boiling, and making *boudin*. . . . Huge marrow-bones might now be seen roasting most temptingly by fires made of *bois de vache,* and a new spirit seemed infused into the entire party by their favorite diet." The animal was only a bull; but the frontiersmen chewed succulent memories with the stringy flesh, and persuaded themselves it was a great feast.

The next day, near the South Fork of the Platte, the expedition saw buffalo from the road for the first time. "The effect upon our hunters, and, in fact, upon the whole party, was that of a sudden and most intense excitement, and a yearning, feverish desire to secure as much as possible of this noble game." Stansbury ordered a halt, and the party remained among the buffaloes this and the following day, taking and packing as much meat as they could; for they did not expect to find buffalo herds again. Nor did they.[6]

The tendency of the buffalo was now to congregate in great herds in the northern and in the southern ranges, leaving the country about the highways of emigration bare except in the months of migration. In the summer of 1853, when the herds had practically deserted the Oregon Trail, the Stevens expedition exploring the possible northern route for a Pacific railroad, at the crossing of the Cheyenne River "ascended to the top of a high hill, and for a great distance ahead every square mile seemed to have a herd of buffalo upon it. Their number was variously estimated by the members of

[6] Howard Stansbury, "Exploration and Survey of the Valley of the Great Salt Lake of Utah," Thirty-Second Congress, Special Session, Senate Document.

the party—some as high as half a million. I do not think it is any exaggeration to set it down at two hundred thousand." [7]

In the fifties some bands of buffalo crossed through the South Pass and grazed along the western slope of the Rockies. Thomas Turnbull, overland traveler of 1852, when on the Carson River in Nevada, wrote laboriously: "along this River is the place to fatten stock quick good feed & water some Buffaloes come here at times plenty Wolves, Crows, Ducks, & Hares." These errant buffalo were quickly exterminated.

From the table-lands that enclosed the valley of the Platte, two to ten miles from the river, the buffaloes had come in single file, in parallel lines about twenty yards apart, to the river banks. In the hundreds of years, innumerable trails had been traced, many of them nearly a foot into the soil. Prairie schooners in clambering over these ruts sometimes broke an axle; and train captains who knew their business had each wagon carry an extra axle to meet the emergency. But the trails, again, were sometimes invaluable compass lines to travelers outside the beaten track. "We left the Platte with its bluffs and cañons behind us, and out into the boundless plains we rode, and only drew rein

[7] Isaac I. Stevens, *Narrative and Final Report of Explorations . . . ,* Part I (Washington, 1855).

[120]

when we discovered that we had lost our reckoning, and were without a compass," was the experience of General Rusling. "Fortunately we had the buffalo trails, that there run almost due north and south . . . they are a sure guide up and down the bluffs, many of which are so precipitous that safe ascent or descent elsewhere seems impossible. But the buffalo, by a wise instinct, seems to have hit just the right path." [8]

Horace Greeley, making his redoubtable overland journey in the summer of 1859, found the buffalo in the Solomon Forks country, on the Pike's Peak Express route. The soil was rich, and matted with their favorite grass; yet, as Greeley put it: "it is all eaten down like an over-taxed sheep-pasture in a dry August." He was rampantly confident that the herd before his eyes contained no less than a million buffaloes.

The stagecoach drivers had had several narrow escapes from being run down by the buffaloes, which grazed on either side of the road and at times ran headlong across it. Mr. Fuller, the superintendent of the division, was riding his mule along the road, when a herd of buffalo, stampeding away from an emigrant train, suddenly galloped across a ridge; the first advice Mr. Fuller had of their presence was when his mule was knocked down and the

[8] J. F. Rusling, *Across America* (New York, 1874, p. 52).

[121]

lead buffalo brushed just past him. The superintendent, huddled against the body of the mule, miraculously escaped from the stampede with only a bruise or two.

Some parties of "Pike's Peakers" experienced the danger of buffalo stampedes in the night. While gunfire swerved the buffalo from the tents, several domestic oxen were swept away in these stampedes. The guards at the stagecoach stations had to keep up a continual watch to prevent the mules from disappearing in a rush of buffaloes.[9]

As the line of heavy traffic swung to the Colorado gold fields, buffalo were more commonly seen on the Platte. Opposite Grand Island was the little town of Wood River Center; in the summer of 1860 the town was almost a stamping ground for the buffalo. In mid-June the editor of the little weekly newspaper reminds his readers that editors are infallible prophets: "As we sometimes since predicted, our beautiful town site has been rudely trampled upon by those ugly-looking wild beasts, known as buffalo. . . . We intend to keep some weapons handy, so that, should they kick up too much dust around our office, or rob the porkers of their accustomed slop, we shall not be responsible for their safety. We are determined not to be *bit* by the ugly scamps, at all hazards, and should the *Echo*

[9] Horace Greeley, *An Overland Journey* (New York, 1860).

A NARROW ESCAPE FROM THE BUFFALOES

From Albert D. Richardson, *Beyond the Mississippi* (American Publishing Company, Hartford, 1867).

fail at any time to make its accustomed visit, it may be inferred that either ourself or some huge buffalo has fallen, and perchance, editor, printer, and devil may have, for the moment, forgotten their duty, whilst regaling upon the finest broiled hump ribs." Next month *The Huntsman's Echo* must report that buffaloes have broken into the garden of one of Wood River Center's most prominent citizens, and eaten his maize crop: "There is a fine herd in sight over towards Prairie Creek as we go to press. . . . A few miles above, on the Platte and Wood rivers, there are numerous herds. Across the river, it is said, they are coming over from the Republican, in innumerable multitudes, and many famishing for food or water." And in the *Echo* for the first week in August there is, inevitably: "The slaughtered carcasses are thickly scattered along the road across the river, the stench from which is fearful to delicate olfactories." [10]

Wagon trains following the Overland Trail in 1862 found no buffaloes near the Fork of the Platte, but thousands of skeletons. Travelers could no longer depend upon the prairie to furnish them meat; and dealers in groceries and liquors had established themselves at various points on the route. "The American Ranche, a Home for the Weary,"

[10] *The Huntsman's Echo,* Wood River Center, Nebraska Territory, 1860: in possession of the Nebraska State Historical Society.

had its card regularly in *The Huntsman's Echo,* announcing that it "Keeps constantly on hand a supply of Groceries and Provisions, Garden Sauce— Can fruit of all kinds, Liquors, Cigars, Corn, Oats —and, in fact, everything to please the Emigrant."

Meanwhile the fur trade continued its toll on the buffalo herds. Fort Benton, Montana, had developed as a rendezvous for traders and Indians. Two thousand buffalo robes had been collected here by the fur companies in 1834; seven years later the annual collection had risen to 20,000 robes; and thence to the outbreak of the Civil War an average of 20,000 robes a year was sent down the river from Fort Benton. The town of Kansas City had developed, to dispute the supremacy of St. Louis as a fur market; 70,400 buffalo robes were received in Kansas City warehouses in the year of 1857, and 55,000 pounds of buffalo meat. The Panic of 1857 did not deter Pierre Chouteau and Company, who flooded the New York market with buffalo robes just as its parent firm had done in the panic of twenty years before. In the summer of 1860 the steamboats *Broad Eagle, Key West,* and *Chippewa* brought 66,000 robes from the upper Missouri posts to the St. Louis fur companies; and from other posts 15,000 robes more were brought to St. Louis.

Within the memory of men still living in this year of 1860, the traveler venturing into the West had made up his outfit and started out, first from Schenectady, New York; then from Clarksburg, Virginia; then from Maysville, Kentucky, and later Kaskaskia, Illinois; then from St. Louis; and now even Leavenworth, Kansas, was sometimes spoken of as "east." The kerosene footlights were being relit, and in a moment the curtain was to creak upwards on the fourth act of the drama. And in the fourth act somebody always gets killed.

CHAPTER VII

CIRCUS IN KANSAS

THE wild life of the buffalo was cut short with a penstroke when in 1862 a bill for the construction of a railroad from the western border of Iowa to San Francisco received the President's signature. Dr. Edwin James forty years before had written of the plains of the West: "We have but little apprehension of giving too unfavorable an account of this portion of the country. . . . The traveller who shall at any time have traversed its desolate sands, will, we think, join us in the wish that this region may remain for ever the unmolested haunt of the native hunter, the bison, and the jackall." But even if the doctor had been right, and the Great American Desert all that New England schoolboys believed of it, the cleaving of the range by the twin steel bands meant that the bison, bulls, cows, and calves would be shot down; that the Indian would not be allowed to remain a hunter, nor even a native; and that the "jackalls" would be poisoned and their skins redeemed for bounties.

In 1865 the actual building of the Union Pacific

Railroad was begun. With its completion the buffaloes in the United States were divided into two great herds, that never joined again: a northern herd of about a million and a half, and a southern herd of nearer five million buffalo. The northern herd ranged through the Powder River country and into British possessions. In the Southwest buffalo were abundant in western Texas; but the favorite feeding ground of the southern herd was the section of the plains about the Republican River, between the Arkansas and the South Platte.

Both herds retreated from the roadway of the Union Pacific, leaving a strip of fifty miles and more barren of any great wild life. When in 1867 Major Powell traveled the Union Pacific to its terminus, then near Cheyenne, he saw during his entire trip only one live buffalo, an old bull wandering aimlessly along the bank of the Platte.

The year the golden spike was driven that completed the laying of the trans-Pacific railway, the Kansas Pacific Railroad was building across Kansas, toward Denver; and the Atchison, Topeka, and Santa Fe was throwing its rails across the wagon ruts of the Santa Fe trail. The southern herd was hacked by the advancing lines of travel, and for seekers of profit or pleasure the way was opened into the heart of the buffalo country.

In the autumn of 1868 this new field for pleasure

seekers was opened up. The buffalo, associated with everything wild and daring, could now be hunted indolently, under the comforting auspices of business-eager railroads. From Cincinnati, Chicago, St. Louis, excursions at low rates were announced. Railway stations bore placards such as this:

RAILWAY EXCURSION
AND
BUFFALO HUNT

An excursion train will leave Leavenworth, at 8 A.M., and Lawrence at 10 A.M., for

Sheridan,

On Tuesday, October 27, 1868, and return on Friday. This train will stop at the principal stations both going and coming. Ample time will be had for a grand Buffalo

HUNT ON THE PLAINS

Buffaloes are so numerous along the road that they are shot from the cars nearly every day On our last excursion our party killed twenty buffaloes in a hunt of six hours.

All passengers can have refreshments on the cars at reasonable prices.

Tickets of round trip from Leavenworth, $10.00.

Phil Sheridan, near the Kansas-Colorado border, was then the "end of the tracks" for the Kansas Pacific railway; but building was going on beyond, and a town was being surveyed for the next terminus—this to be complimentarily named Kit Carson.

Sheridan was the terminus for a year and a half, and developed into the most flagrant variety of a hell-roaring railroad town, with gamblers, horse thieves, murderers, and many gaudy ladies among its population of two thousand—with Metropolitan Bars, Imperial Hotels, and Palace Ballrooms, occasionally with whiffs of gunsmoke blending into the other unsavory odors of these public buildings—and, before its course was run, a Committee of Safety, and posted warnings for various ladies and gentlemen to leave town within forty-eight hours. The honor of being the terminus carried with it a substantial freighting trade, with bull trains and mules bearing merchandise to Colorado and New Mexico and returning with wool, ores, and buffalo hides.

East of Sheridan, trains might flank herds of bison spreading far over the plains. The buffalo had not yet learned to take flight at sight of the engines; if buffalo were traveling in a course across the railway, away they went, charging across the ridge on which the iron rails lay, determined to head off the locomotive and cross in front of it. It often happened that buffaloes and cars ran side by side for a mile or two, so near that passengers could almost clutch the buffalo by their manes; then the car windows were opened, and breechloaders flung hundreds of wanton bullets.

THE FRONTIER IN '69

Title page of W. E. Webb, *Buffalo Land* (E. Hannaford, Chicago and Cincinnati, 1872).

The daily train was a "mixed" affair, with freight cars carrying quartermasters' stores or goods for the railroad commissary, and sometimes stock cars bringing remounts for cavalrymen, preceding one or two passenger cars. It left Lawrence for the west at ten in the morning, and speeding at fifteen to twenty miles an hour continued through the monotonous plains. During the day the train passed Fort Riley, an old army post stranded in a district where there were no longer any savages, and reduced in dignity to a stockade for antiquated cavalry horses.

Farther west the train passed Abilene—"a hotel, a few shanties, and a number of cars upon a side track"—a small town that was to batten on cattle droves brought across unfenced ranges up the Chisholm Trail from Texas.

As dusk came on, a single straggling buffalo or a small herd of antelope might be seen. The train was at the fringe of the buffalo country.

At eight in the evening the train arrived at Ellsworth. Farther west there might be Indian war parties; and on this account, in the autumn of 1868, the Kansas Pacific ran beyond Ellsworth only in daylight. The passengers were, accordingly, "booked for the night." Ellsworth boasted a hotel, the Anderson House, that could accommodate some of the passengers; others were billeted on the citizenry, or sprawled out in the cars. Rudolph Keim, going westward to join Phil Sheridan, the commandant-general of the department, enjoyed Room Number One of the Anderson House, but he has left a doubtful endorsement: "After a supper on buffalo steak, antelope ham, soggy bread, and a cup of warm water, flavored with a grain of coffee or a leaf of tea, the passengers gathered in the hotel office, a small room eight by ten and furnished with a counter and several dilapidated chairs. The proprietor presided. Seating himself on a three legged chair and cocking his feet on the stove," he entertained them with yarns laudatory of his own career, and bits of the red-rich history of Ellsworth in the days when it was the railroad terminus.[1] Since the railroad had pushed farther west, the town had—the landlord said—become quite orderly. Keim complains of "violent yells" and "salvos of uproarious oaths" throughout the night, but the landlord seems to have been right—there was no shooting.

At daybreak the train was ready to depart; that event was announced just in time to allow a last round of drinks, and "with a parting benediction upon the landlord's head most of the passengers retired to an adjacent rum mill and stowed

[1] R. de B. Keim, *Sheridan's Troopers on the Border* (Philadelphia, 1855); Colonel H. W. Wheeler, *The Frontier Trail* (Los Angeles, 1923).

away a slug or two of mountain dew to keep up their spirits."

The locomotive whistled "up brakes," and snorted out of Ellsworth. The luxuriant prairie grass found farther eastward gave way to the stubby, deep-rooted buffalo grass. An occasional woodpile or watertank, watched by a squad of soldiers, with a dilapidated freight car for their sleeping quarters, was the only kind of railway station.

As the morning brightened, Rudolph Keim could see small herds of buffalo, indefinite spots along the horizon. In the car in which he was seated were twenty-five stand of arms, breech-loading rifles, and a chest of needle cartridges, provided by the Kansas Pacific for its employees. Each passenger carried his own arms.

Suddenly shots rang out from the forward car; the trainmen rushed to the rifle rack and armed themselves. "At this juncture as I thought things were getting serious I re-examined my own rifle, buckled on a pair of pistols, slung my cartridge-box over my shoulder and started forward to look into the cause of the commotion. At this moment a shout 'Buffalo crossing the track!' was heard and bang! bang! bang! simultaneously went several pieces. Poking my head out of the window I observed a small herd of six buffalo bulls running at full speed parallel with the train, and about a hundred yards ahead and not more than sixty feet from the track." They seemed bent upon crossing, but finding the locomotive pursuing too closely, they swerved away. Instantly the engineer slackened the speed of the train, to accommodate the fusiliers. The barrage wounded two of the buffalo; the locomotive whistled "down brakes," and without waiting for the train to stop every one, passengers, engineer, conductor, brakeman, jumped off the cars and gave chase.

One of the wounded buffaloes was still on his feet, "and with great effort was trying to escape. He had been shot in the thigh and though retarded made good progress, when another ball taking effect in the other leg, let his hind quarters down upon the ground. Nothing daunted the wounded animal made every exertion to drag himself off, on his two fore feet, when a ball under his shoulder put an end to his suffering and his efforts to rejoin his companions. A cheer wound up the railroad chase, when the busy knives of 'professionals' in hip-joint operations, soon had the 'rumps' severed and after cutting out the tongues and a few strips of 'hump' the rest of the two immense carcasses was left as a dainty and abundant repast for the wolf. The meat was put on the train, and again we continued our journey."

About noon the train reached Hays City, the

shell of a railroad town; all the restless spirits had moved on to Phil Sheridan station, a hundred miles away.

Past Hays City the train carried few passengers —these fierce, hirsute, and unwashed. The conductor buckled his pistol belt about his waist, and kept his rifle near him.

Large herds of buffalo were now to be seen; and thirty miles from Hays City the prairie was blackened with them.

"A number of smaller herds which had crossed to the south upon the approach of the train," recorded a passenger, "invariably raised their heads, looked at us for an instant, and then with heads down and tails up galloped across ahead of the locomotive. In trying this strategic feat one specimen found himself forcibly lifted into the air and thrown into the ditch, where he lay upon his back, his cloven feet flourishing madly.

"Several animals had been shot from the car out of this herd. The train now stopped to afford time to bring in a few rumps. While this operation was going on, a party of six or eight of us started down the track to dispatch the buffalo, still kicking and bellowing with a mixture of suspense and rage. When our party got within fifty yards a shot was fired which seemed to have a peculiarly vitalizing effect. With one desperate bound the old beast regained his feet. Several more shots were instantly fired, but none seemed to take effect. Instead of retreating the irate quadruped made for our party, coming at a full jump, head down, tongue out, bleeding and frothing at the mouth, eyes flashing, and to cap the climax of his terrible exhibition of infuriation, roared fearfully. As there was no time to lose, and to fire at him 'head on' would be a waste of ammunition, the party scattered in all directions. For my own part, I took occasion to make a few long and rapid strides across the track into the ditch on the other side. The rest of the party imitated this dexterous movement without many moments of reflection. Losing sight of us, the enraged animal, smarting under the blow he had received from the locomotive, and the tickling he had sustained from our rifles, reaped his anger upon the opposite side of the embankment of the railroad by rending great furrows in the earth, stamping on the ground, raising a great dust, and making a terrible noise. Raising up so as to get a partial sight of his carcass, not over thirty feet off, three of our party fired, the rest holding in reserve. Every ball seemed to take effect. Almost instantly the animal fell upon his knees. The rest then fired, when the animal rolled completely over. One deep gasp, a convulsive motion of the jaws, one sudden flash of the eye. . . ."

For sixty miles the same great multitudes of buffalo were in sight. As the train approached Sheridan the herd thinned out to isolated bulls, until even they disappeared. At six in the evening the train drew up at tracks' end—where a wooden milepost announced "405 to S. L.," 405 miles to the state line at Kansas City. The heart of the buffalo country had been cut through.

In 1870 it seemed that survivors of the smaller herds had joined the single great herd; and when this southern herd crossed the tracks in front of the locomotive, trains had to wait for hours. Engineers tried the experiment of running through the buffalo, but after their engines had been thrown from the track they learned to give a closely massed herd the right of way.

Passengers to Denver and Salt Lake, on the Smoky Hill route of the Union Pacific, had frequent opportunities of shooting at buffalo from the windows and platforms of the cars.

Twice in one week trains of the Santa Fe were thrust from the tracks by buffalo. An army officer remembered an occasion in 1871 or 1872, when "the train entered a large herd, which scattered and seemed to go wild at the shrieking of the whistle and the ringing of the bell. As we went on the thicker they became, until the very earth appeared to be a rolling mass of humps as far as we could see. Suddenly some of the animals nearest us turned and charged; others fell in behind, and down on us they came like an avalanche. The engineer stopped the engine, let off steam and whistled to stop them, while we fired from the platforms and windows. We stood in the center of the car to avert the crash. On they came, the earth trembling, and plunged heads down into us. Some were wedged in between the cars, others beneath; and so great was the crash that they topped three cars over and actually scrambled over them, one buffalo becoming bogged by having his legs caught in the window." [2]

It was as hunter for the construction gang of the Kansas Pacific that William Frederick Cody, Buffalo Bill himself, attained his prominence and his title.

Engaged, incidentally, in destroying the game-range, the crews depended on the buffalo for meat as construction extended into the plains. The Kansas Pacific employed a construction gang of twelve hundred men; and the commissariat relied largely upon several buffalo hunters. Cody was one of these. His contract called upon him to kill an average of twelve buffaloes daily, oversee the cutting and dressing of the meat, and look after its transportation;

[2] Charles F. Holder, "The Crime of a Century," *Harper's Weekly*, LXXXI; T. H. Davis, "The Buffalo Range," *Harper's Monthly*, XXXVIII.

BUFFALO BILL

From W. E. Webb, *Buffalo Land* (E. Hannaford, Chicago and Cincinnati, 1872).

for this he was to receive five hundred dollars a month. The pay was large because the Indian and the buffalo had retreated from the roadway in company, and there was no assurance of locating a kill without finding a fight.

Cody's equipment was a trained buffalo horse by the name of Brigham, and a heavy-shooting, breech-loading needle gun.

Once, when the cry went up that a herd of buffalo was coming toward the camp, Cody mounted his horse without waiting to saddle him, and galloped toward the game. He found five other hunters waiting for the herd—a captain and four lieutenants from the near-by post, Fort Harker. The captain graciously told the young man that they intended to kill a few buffalo for sport, that all they intended to take away were the tongues and a chuck of the tenderloin, and that the young fellow could have all the rest. Cody was properly appreciative.

When the herd—eleven buffaloes in all—came within a few hundred feet, Cody rode out from the party, circled, and came upon the buffalo from the rear. One shot from the needle gun, and the rear buffalo was dead; and the trained horse immediately galloped beside the next. With twelve shots, all eleven buffalo were killed. The officers had not even had a shot at the game. When the sense of their disappointment had passed, they were enthusiastic. They dubbed Cody with the star-spangled title that he carried proudly through life, and circulated the anecdote.

The friends of Billy Comstock, chief of scouts at Fort Wallace, were indignant that there should be another Buffalo Bill on the range, and demanded a contest for the title.

The stage for the circus was fixed upon twenty miles east of Sheridan. A side bet of $500 between the two claimants was announced. Considerable publicity was given the affair. The Kansas Pacific carried an excursion party from St. Louis for the exhibition. Officers, soldiers, railroad men, plainsmen took the day off to be present.

Referees were assigned to follow each man and tally his slain buffalo.

The two hunters rode side by side until a herd was sighted and the word given, when they dashed off, separating to the right and left. Cody, by killing the leaders of his part of the herd, pressed the others into a running circle, from which he picked off the buffalo in quick succession. Comstock rode after his, killing the rearmost animal each time. Cody killed thirty-eight, Comstock twenty-three. The hunters and referees retraced their way past the carcasses to the cheering crowd, and the spectators and performers took luncheon. The cake was hardly eaten when another herd was sighted, a bunch of cows and their calves. Score: Cody eighteen, Comstock fourteen.

A third herd shortly appeared. Cody pulled the saddle off Brigham, and rode bareback to the hunt. He killed sixty-nine buffalo while Comstock was killing fifty-seven. When Cody came to his last buffalo, he headed the bull toward the company of spectators; and as the ladies were frightened into lusty screams, Brigham gained the side of the buffalo at a bound, Cody sent a ball through the hide, and the animal rolled into the dust at the very feet of the spectators.[3]

In eighteen months as buffalo hunter for the construction crew Cody killed 4,280 buffalo.

The heads of the buffaloes slain in the Cody-Comstock hunt were mounted by the Kansas Pacific and distributed about the country. In one way, it was dubious advertising; for Cody's nonchalant bang-banging exploded the legend of "sport" in buffalo hunting on horseback and with heavy guns. Cody's performance suggested all too strongly that buffalo hunting as a sport combined the amusement of a midway sporting gallery with the hazard to life and limb of a Chicago stockyard corral.

But sport was no longer the attraction of the hunt by the time the Kansas Pacific was completed.

[3] William F. Cody, *Life of Buffalo Bill, by Himself* (Hartford, 1879).

The attraction was the money. Hunting trips for the fun of it were not given up, however, simply because by 1871 professional buffalo hunters began their domination of the range.

Conductors on the Kansas Pacific could tell the would-be hunter at what point on the line the buffalo chanced then to be the most numerous. Several stations west of Ellsworth offered usually equal opportunities for hunting. Russell was particularly attractive, if the buffalo happened to be numerous along the eastern part of the range, for there was a hotel at Russell. Most other stations offered no better accommodations than a few dugouts. Horses could be obtained at Ellsworth, or Russell, or Hays City; and sportsmen preferred to hunt on horseback, for the sense of excitement it gave. A natty carbine breechloader with a twelve-cartridge magazine could be obtained, that hung by a strap from the shoulders. A rider with such a gun dangling across his saddle could draw his revolvers, and after using both have his rifle in reserve: he could fire twenty-four shots without the bother of reloading.

It was best, of course, for the hunter to discover the direction of the wind before he reached the herd; but perhaps due to the many confusing scares that buffaloes now encountered, they seemed to be losing their keenness of smell.

If the hunter was well advised he took advantage

of the ravines and the depressions between the billows of the plain in nearing the buffalo. It was an egregious blunder to go dashing over the prairie for a half mile in full view of the game.

Say that the hunter discovered, not over two hundred yards in front of him, a lone bull. The buffalo's broad nostrils suddenly caught a whiff of the tainted breeze. The hunter was still invisible in the tall grass of the ravine, but the buffalo was instantly in flight—directly into the teeth of the wind, with the hunter forcing his mount in pursuit.

"I looked at the little carbine in my hand, and then at the magnificent spectacle of the huge animal at bay, unscathed and robust in the wildest beauty, and in my heart I could have been contented with the splendid picture before me, and have permitted the warrior to have gone back to his sweet-breathed kine upon the plains." Yes indeed!

The hunter breathed in an atmosphere muskish-tainted by the game ahead. The up-and-down canter of the buffalo, tossing its mane about, and gaining in appearance from the height of the hump, made the lumbering animal seem terrifyingly huge.

"Put in your spurs, comrade; don't spare. Get up beside him as quickly as possible. Once there, the horse will easily stick. A stern chase disheartens the pursuer, encourages the pursued. Look out for that creek! See how the buffalo takes the steep bank—a

THE VANQUISHED FOE

From Grantley F. Berkeley, *The English Sportsman in the Western Prairies* (Hurst and Blackett, London, 1861).

plunge headlong, which sends the dust up in clouds. Now, as we check and turn into a ford, he is going up the opposite side. Another hundred yards, and we are close behind him. The long tongue is hung out, and his head lies low down, as he plunges forward, diverging ever so little as we press up opposite his foreshoulders. That was a bad shot, my friend, barely missing your horse's head."

Some of the bullets were telling; the hunter could hear them crack into the buffalo's hide. There was a red spot above a lung, and blood oozing over the jaws. Now the buffalo slackened his pace for a more even canter; then, swinging about and facing the horse and rider, he made a sudden vicious charge. The horse came well out of the way, by a tug at the rein or by his own sense; and the buffalo jarred himself into a halt. The wound at his side was sputtering red globules; the beard was crimsoning; the eyes were swollen with pain and anger.

Gradually, doubling his legs under him, the buffalo sank to his stomach. Without a premonitory motion he tumbled on his side; and his legs stretched out and stiffened. The flesh, except the tongue, wasn't worth the bother of taking, of course; but the head would make a splendid trophy, if the hunter could get a wagon to pick it up.

When the *London Field* devoted the "leader" of one of its 1876 issues to deploring the pending extermination of the buffalo in America ("The disappearance . . . will be a scandal to civilization, and a subject for undying shame and remorse to the children of the men who did nothing to stay the hand of the destroyer"), the American *Cultivator and Country Gentleman* editorially wiped away a crocodile tear, and thought it "not unjust nor discourteous" to add that parties of English sportsmen had been particularly ruthless slaughterers of the buffalo.

William Frederick Cody was once paid a thousand dollars a month to act as guide on a buffalo-hunting trip for an English gentleman with a few guests.

In 1872 the Grand Duke Alexis, of Russia, was visiting America. Having been wined and dined in the eastern states to a surfeit, he expressed a wish to see the native wild life of America—the Indian and the buffalo in their Plains home.

General Sheridan managed the western tour, with Buffalo Bill as his active assistant. With the aid of Spotted Tail, the Sioux chief, he presented the Grand Duke with the spectacle of an Indian war dance. The Sioux staged also an Indian buffalo hunt; the warrior Two-Lance was there, to send an arrow entirely through the body of a buffalo bull running at full speed—a feat that no other Sioux then alive could accomplish.

Alexis asked Cody a great many questions about

the sport of killing buffalo. Buffalo Bill offered the use of his trained buffalo horse, Buckskin Joe, if the Grand Duke wished to try for himself. Early the next morning, accordingly, the party were in their saddles and galloping over the prairies in search of a buffalo herd.

Once buffaloes were in sight the Grand Duke was greatly excited, and Cody had to restrain him from charging at the buffaloes forthwith. By keeping behind sand hills the two approached the herd; and once in the open they tore after the buffaloes.

Within a hundred yards of the animals the Duke fired and missed. Cody rode close to his side and directed him to hold his fire until he was directly upon the buffalo. The two hunters dashed off together, and ran their horses beside either flank of a large bull; and Alexis fired a fatal shot. When his retinue came up there were congratulations, and his good health was drunk in champagne. The Grand Duke had no more worlds to conquer; and he ordered a return to the railroad.

CHAPTER VIII

THE BUSINESS OF BUFFALO HUNTING

TRAVELERS along the Arkansas River in 1870 passed through herds of buffaloes for two hundred miles, almost one continuous gathering, as close together as it was customary to herd cattle at a round-up. Robert Wright wrote of this great herd: "When, at nightfall, they came to the river, particularly when it was in flood, their immense numbers, in their headlong plunge, would make you think, by the thunderous noise, that they had dashed all the water from the river." The chosen abode of the buffalo was rich in smaller wild life—birds as well as quadrupeds. About Dodge City in southern Kansas, established in 1872, there was in its first year and for several years after a multitude of game fowl —ducks, geese, swans, brants, pelicans—on its streams and ponds. "It was a poor day or a poor hunter who could not kill a hundred ducks and geese in a day, and sometimes several hundred were killed in a day," an old resident recalled. "The turkeys and quails—there was no end to them. I have seen thousands of turkeys in a flock, coming in to roost on the North Fork and the main Canadian and its timbered branches. Several times, at a distance, we mistook them for large herds of buffalo. They literally covered the prairie for miles."

In May of 1871 Colonel Dodge drove in a buggy from Fort Zara to Fort Larned, thirty-four miles, along the Arkansas River. At least twenty-five miles of that journey was through one immense herd. From a distance it appeared one solid black mass moving slowly northward, and it was only when Colonel Dodge was actually among them that he could recognize that the apparently solid mass was made up of countless small herds of from fifty to two hundred animals in each. As long as he was in the broad river valley, the herds sullenly got out of his way, and turned, within thirty or fifty yards, to stare. When, however, he approached the low line of hills that culminates in Pawnee Rock, the buffaloes at the crest of the herd took alarm at the unusual object in their rear, and stampeded at full speed toward the traveler.

Fortunately for the colonel, his horse was a veteran of buffalo hunts, and stood quietly. Reining him up, Dodge waited until the front mass of the plunging herd was within fifty yards; then, with a few sure shots, he dropped some of the leaders, and the herd swerved to either side of the wedge of fallen bodies. When all had passed the buggy they stopped, apparently perfectly satisfied, although thousands were yet within rifle reach. After Dodge's aide had cut out the tongues of the fallen leaders, he proceeded on his journey, only to have exactly the same experience within another mile or two.

But already cattle and cowboys were advancing from south Texas into the buffalo country. While buffaloes in countless thousands were roaming western Kansas, in 1868 at Abilene, in eastern Kansas, there arrived fully seventy-five thousand cattle from the Texas prairies—most to be shipped eastward to the slaughterhouses, but many of them to stock the Kansas range. Buffaloes were used, with a sad humor that no one remarked, to advertise the greatness of Abilene as a cattle market. Jim McCoy, the mayor of Abilene, hit upon the scheme of sending a carload of wild buffaloes east, covering the sides of the car with advertisements of the semimonthly sales of stock cattle at Abilene. The Kansas Pacific furnished a reënforced cattle car, which was sidetracked at Fossil Creek in western Kansas, and a party of seven horsemen, three or four of them Texas cowboys and the rest California Spaniards, set out to capture buffalo alive. In two days ten full-grown buffaloes were lassoed, and pulled into the car up an inclined plane by a block-and-tackle arrangement. Four of them died from anger added to the heat of the car, before they were moved from the sidetrack. The car, with flaming advertisements painted in canvas on its sides, was sent to St. Louis and thence to Chicago, getting as much attention and publicity as the sponsors could have hoped for. At Chicago the buffalo were turned upon the enclosed commons of the stockyards, and after being exhibited there for a few days were killed. The hides were presented to a "professor," a veterinary surgeon, who had the skins stuffed and sent to London.

In north Texas by 1869 cattle herds had claimed much of the buffalo range. Occasionally buffaloes stampeded into the cattle, and swept many of the kine away with them. Getting cattle out of a herd of buffalo was exciting sport for cowboys. An outfit that included Jim McIntire, later one of the best-known buffalo hunters, once spent two weeks in reclaiming cattle from buffalo herds, and succeeded in combing out about two thousand of them.

Early in 1870 one John Wright Mooar, a young fellow fascinated by tales of the grandeur and the dangers of the Wild West, left New York City and came to Fort Hays, Kansas. He got a contract to supply the army post with wood, and stayed. Here he became familiar with one James White, who made his living selling buffalo meat to the post commissary. The hides of the buffaloes he killed he threw away.

Mooar suggested that they try to find a market for the hides. They shipped twenty-one to Mooar's brother in New York; but he could make no sale of them, and ultimately gave the hides to a Pennsylvania tannery. The tanners experimented, were satisfied, and contracted with the Mooar brothers and White for two thousand hides at three dollars and a half each.

Other tanners, English and American, soon entered the market, one English tannery contracting for ten thousand hides in its first order. Agents came to Hays City and offered prices that made buffalo hunting a good business. The killing of buffalo for their hides was commenced on a large scale, and the slaughter was on.

Unless one owned a ranch, the quickest way to make money on the frontier was to turn buffalo hunter. In 1870 bull hides brought two dollars each, and cowhides and calf hides twenty-five cents less. The tongues, salted and packed in barrels, brought good side money; and the "mop," the bunch of long hair that fell over the buffalo's horns and eyes, was worth seventy-five cents a pound. Many hunters were too anxious to run up their number of hides to take the time to attend to these side lines.

The largest collectors of buffalo robes and hides by 1870 were Bates, of St. Louis, and Durfee, of Leavenworth, Kansas. In a single year the collections of these two firms amounted to over two hundred thousand skins.

Two-thirds of the robes found their way to New York. In 1870 New York dealers, buying by the hundred-pack, paid about sixteen dollars and a half for a grade-A "seasonable" robe, and thirteen dollars and eight dollars for second-grade and third-grade skins. These prices tumbled as pot-hunters in wagons, horseback, and afoot, poured into the buffalo range.

"Think," advertisers sentimentally exhorted readers, "as you tuck the warm robe about you for your joyous sleigh-ride, the winter skin of the bison was once the very best clothes of a roamer over the Buffalo Range." The demand for buffalo robes and for coats of buffalo fur expanded with the supply. Summer skins were wanted by manufacturers for machinery belting and for other leather uses. This dual demand meant that buffalo hunting might be followed for the twelve months of the year; that the summer respite, the immunity during the rutting season that the Indians and the old fur traders had allowed the buffalo, was a privilege of the past.

By 1871 meat packers were interested in the buffalo as food. Buffalo meat attained popularity as a novelty in the East, and the market for buffalo tongues became steady. But the butchers' trade in buffalo was most successful, divertingly enough, in selling the steaks clandestinely as domestic beef to customers who never knew the difference. Buffalo steak was commonly served at all the western railway eating houses and at the western hotels. A. C. Myers built a smokehouse on Pawnee Fork, where he cured hams for eastern markets. The meat was prepared by dividing each of the hindquarters into three chunks, which were sugar-cured, smoked, and sewn into canvas. This was choice meat, and commanded a good price.

The merchants of the little towns along the railroads were not slow to snatch advantage of the boom in hunting. Many of them became rich in advancing outfits of guns, ammunition, and stores to buffalo hunters, on an ordinary credit arrangement or on a stated percentage of the hides taken.

The largest buffalo-skin tannery ever built was at Greeley, Colorado. There tens of thousands of the finest of buffalo robes were tied up in huge bales and stacked high in piles for shipment.[1]

Wright, Beverly and Company developed an immense business at Dodge City. Charlie Rath and Bob Wright shipped over two hundred thousand hides the first winter the Atchison, Topeka and Santa Fe reached Dodge City, and other dealers shipped almost as many from there, besides two hun-

[1] John L. Cowan, "The Trail of the Hide Hunter," *Outing*, LIX.

dred cars of hind quarters and two cars of buffalo tongues. The editor of the Dodge City newspaper gave the company a free "write-up" in an issue of 1877: "In their warehouse and yard, it is no uncommon thing to find from sixty to eighty thousand buffalo robes and hides. This house also does a banking business for the accommodation of its customers. Mr. John Newton, the portly and benevolent *charge de affairs* of the office, will accommodate you with five dollars or five thousand dollars, as the case may be. We generally get the former amount. Mr. Samuels, who has special charge of the shooting irons and jewelry stock, will entertain you in Spanish, German, Russian, or Hebrew. The assistance of Mr. Isaacson, the clothier, is demanded for *parle vous,* while Bob Wright, himself, has to be called on when the dusky and dirty 'child of the setting sun' insists on spouting Cheyenne and Arapahoe and goes square back on the King's English. They employed over a dozen outside men to check off the wagons that were loading, and their sales were on an average of a thousand dollars a day, Sundays not excepted, or three hundred and fifty thousand dollars a year, and several years it was over four hundred thousand dollars." [2] Of course, the interest of Wright, Beverly and Company extended beyond the

[2] *Ford County Globe* quoted, Robert Wright, *Dodge City, the Cowboy Capital* (n. p. 1913), p. 158.

trade in buffalo skins. There was almost nothing, the proprietors boasted, that they did not handle.

William Blackmore, English sportsman, reviewing these years, wrote: "When in the West in 1872, I satisfied myself by personal inquiries that the number of buffalo being then annually slaughtered for their hides was at least one million per annum. In the autumn of 1868, whilst crossing the plains on the Kansas Pacific Railroad—for a distance of upwards of 120 miles, between Ellsworth and Sheridan, we passed through an almost unbroken herd of buffalo. The Plains were blackened with them, and more than once the train had to stop to allow unusually large herds to pass. A few years afterwards, when traveling over the same line of railroad, it was a rare sight to see a few herds of from ten to twenty buffalo. A like result took place still further southwards, between the Arkansas and Cimmaron rivers. In 1872, whilst on a scout for about a hundred miles south of Fort Dodge to the Indian Territory, we were never out of sight of buffalo. In the following autumn, while traveling over the same district, whilst the whole country was whitened with bleached and bleaching bones, we did not meet with buffalo until we were well into the Indian country, and then only in scanty bands. During this autumn, when riding some thirty or forty miles along the north bank of the Arkansas River to the east of Fort

Dodge, there was a continuous line of putrescent carcasses, so that the air was rendered pestilential and offensive to the last degree. The hunters had formed a line of camps along the banks of this river, and had shot down the buffalo, night and morning, as they came down to drink." [3]

In 1873, when the settlers in eastern Kansas were suffering from the destruction of their crops by the ravages of the grasshoppers, the Army sent several companies to the Republican River valley to kill buffalo for the starving families. When the soldiers arrived at the hunting grounds, however, there was very little meat for them to kill, as the buffalo hunters had slaughtered nearly every buffalo in the district.

Most of the big outfits were operating at first in western Kansas; but in the spring of 1872 a number of hunters ventured into the Texas Panhandle, above the Canadian. The Indians were ready and hostile, and the hunters retired. They doubled back and came into the southern buffalo range from the west, through a trackless wilderness, through herds of antelope, droves of deer, and packs of wolves. But the great game country of the Panhandle was for the most part left alone until the country north of it had been completely ravished.

[3] William Blackmore, Preface to R. I. Dodge, *Plains of the Great West* (New York, 1877).

When construction work on the Santa Fe was stopped in the fall of 1872, hundreds of men were stranded in the Plains without work. All the men who could rustle a team and horses on their own account or could get a merchant to stake them to an outfit became buffalo hunters. During the fall and winter of 1872-73 there were more buffalo hunters on the range than ever before or afterwards. The result was gigantic overproduction; the price of hides and meat threatened to melt away entirely. When the market was worse glutted, hides sold for seventy-five cents each and meat could bring only a half-cent a pound. The small returns frightened many of the newcomers from the field, and prices quickly bounded upwards again.

The fall of 1873 saw an accession of many "hard cases" from the East, who wanted the excitement and the profits of buffalo hunting; but by that time the western merchants, thanks to their credit system, had the business pretty well in hand. The large, well-organized hunting parties were nearly all sent out by them. Central stations were established in the range itself, and smoking houses were built to preserve the meat when it was still fresh from the slaughter.

The most approved party consisted of four men —one shooter, two skinners, and one man to cook, stretch hides, and take care of camp. A light wagon, drawn by two horses or mules, took the outfit into the wilderness, and was sent out each day from camp to bring in the skins upon the field. The supplies were small; the meat of the buffalo was to be the hunters' mainstay. A sack of flour, five pounds of coffee, ten pounds of sugar, a little salt, a side of bacon, and a few pounds of beans, was a month's supply store. Besides the guns and the ammunition, the wagon carried a "Dutch oven," a frying pan, a coffeepot, four tin plates, and four tin cups. The fastidious could impale their food on their skinning knives; the democrats used their fingers. There was also in the wagon a ten-gallon keg of water.

When John Jacobs and John Poe set out as partners in buffalo hunting—"we expected to be buffalo hunters all our lives"—they took two wagons, with two teams of mules, an ox team of four yoke to make occasional trips to trading posts for supplies. They had with them four skinners and two men to stretch the hides. The wagons carried one ton of ammunition—sixteen hundred pounds of lead, and four hundred pounds of powder—besides shells, paper caps, and other accessories.[4] Good hunters did not buy many shells, but refilled the cartridges themselves. The shells of old ammunition seemed to sweat, and often the whole charge of powder would be found in one solid lump. "We used to put fifty

[4] John Jacobs, "Last of the Buffalo," *World's Work,* XVII.

to eighty pounds of lead in a large skillet and get a good blue heat on it. Then we would dip out the lead with a spoon and mold our bullets. Any ball with the least bit of a flaw we put back in the heat."

Anything in the shape of a rifle could be bought in the West—old Kentucky muzzle-loaders, "five feet long in the barrel," condemned Spencer army rifles; Springfield muskets, Henry and Winchester rifles; and the Sharp's "buffalo guns." Knowing hunters chose the Sharp's rifle. These guns, .50 or .55 calibre and weighing about fourteen pounds, firing a heavy charge, would kill at fifteen hundred yards. These rifles were preëminent until in the early eighties, when they were superseded by a new Sharp's rifle, .45 calibre; a hammerless model.[5]

Those who preferred a carbine gun found the short Spencer very effective; it shot "heavy lead," and could be refired rapidly. The carbine was frequently used without bringing it to the shoulder— shot as it rested across the saddle in front of the hunter. This was the old style of hunting the buffalo, when breech-loaders were unknown, and the best gun for buffalo hunting was a short muzzle-loading rifle of large bore. With such a weapon the hunter dispensed with a ramrod; he charged his

[5] George O. Shields, "Buffalo Hunting on the Texas Plains," *Outing,* XI; Harlan B. Kaufmann, "Hunting the Buffalo," *Overland Monthly,* n. s. LXVI.

GOING AFTER AMMUNITION

From W. E. Webb, *Buffalo Land* (E. Hannaford, Chicago and Cincinnati, 1872).

gun simply by pouring the powder down the barrel, and dropping a bullet from his cartridge bag—or his mouth—into the gun, then "sending it home" by sharply striking the butt of the rifle upon his thigh or upon the pommel of his saddle.

Old hunters, expert horsemen, sometimes killed buffalo with lances similar to those used by the Indians; but this was done more for bravado than for any other reason, and was no more typical of the ordinary ways of a buffalo hunter than the rodeo variety of steer-throwing is typical of a cowboy's daily work.

The outfit went where the range was best and buffaloes were most plentiful. A dugout was built and occupied as a permanent camp. "The only kind of a dugout worth having was one with a big, open fire-place, near the edge of a stream with good water, with plenty of wood on its banks. We often occupied the same dugout for a month or more. Then, as buffaloes grew less plentiful, we shifted our camp."

The chase on horseback was too slow and unfruitful a method for the buffalo hunter. Sport be damned; he wanted as many buffalo skins as he could possibly get.

At daylight the hunter started out on foot, carrying his heavy Sharp's gun, with sixty to a hundred cartridges in his belts or his pockets, and a wiping rod. Hanging from his belt was a flat leather scabbard, holding a ripping knife, a hunting knife, and sometimes a butcher's stell on which to whet them.

It was the best of luck to find a herd of from twenty to seventy buffalo in a secluded hollow, where it was possible to make a kill without disturbing any other herd on the range, and where the hunter could skulk between ridges to approach the buffalo very close before he was detected by the herd.

"As the first precaution we always picked up a few blades of dry grass, and let them sift through our fingers. This gives you the true course of the wind, for if Mr. Buffalo ever gets his wind on you his hide is lost for good."

If there were no protecting ridges, the hunter started for the buffalo in a straight line. So long as the hunter's course was straight, up to a distance of about four hundred yards, the buffalo were unsuspecting; but if the hunter took one step to the side, the clumsy eyes of the buffalo were aroused, and the herd was away at a gallop. "There were usually two to four sentinels on the lookout. When they began to get uneasy, we would go down to the ground with more caution if possible and crawl on all fours in a bee-line for the herd and, when the sentinels began to get uneasy again, we knew that our time was up. We were then usually at a distance of from two to three hundred yards."

The hunter, lying on the ground, secured a comfortable rest for his huge rifle, estimated the distance, adjusted his sights, and brought down the hammer on the cap. He aimed at the most suspicious of the watching buffaloes on the rim of the herd—or, if the herd were in motion already, at the buffalo in the lead.

At the first crack of his "pizen slinger" the hunter jumped to his feet and ran after the buffalo. They usually ran from fifty to a hundred feet at the first shot, and a speedy pursuer could go half that distance in the same time. "Then we would drop down and lam it into the first broad side we saw. Then we would have to jump up and run again. This time they would run not quite so far nor so fast, and after we repeated this game a few times we could hold our own with them."

There was some danger in this running, for the hunter had to pass by the first buffaloes he had shot, and sometimes the sight of the hunter brought them to their feet; but a second shot was usually all that they needed.

The vital spot of a buffalo—his heart—was to be reached by a shot fired from a point a little in his rear, the hunter aiming just behind the shoulder blade, and about two-thirds down from the top of the hump. A single shot well placed was quite enough to bring down the most formidable old bull. With the most accurate hunting rifle ever made—the Sharp's gun—and a large mark within easy range, a good hunter could make nearly every shot bring down a mortally wounded buffalo. But the old hunters believed: "A buffalo will not die as long as he is angry."

If the herd was at rest, the hunter might make a "stand"—his most precious maneuver. The leader of the herd was the one to be shot down first. "The noise startles the buffaloes, they stare at the little cloud of white smoke and feel inclined to run, but seeing their leader hesitate they wait for her. She, when struck, gives a violent start forward, but soon stops, and the blood begins to run from her nostrils in two crimson streams. In a couple of minutes her body sways unsteadily, she staggers, tries hard to keep her feet, but soon gives a lurch sideways and falls. Some of the other members of the herd come around her and stare and sniff in wide-eyed wonder, and one of the more wary starts to lead the herd away. But before she takes a dozen steps 'bang!' goes the hidden rifle again, and her leadership is ended forever. Her fall only increases the bewilderment of the survivors over a proceeding which to them is strange and unaccountable, because the danger is not visible. They cluster about the fallen ones, sniff at the warm blood, bawl aloud in wonderment, and do everything but run away." Then the hunter could calmly pick them off, shooting unhurriedly and surely.

John Cook, on the southwest plains, once made a stand—the biggest killing of all his three years' hunting.[6]

It was about midday, in the latter part of June. A herd of several hundred buffalo had been bombarded from the Beaver Creek waters, and the hot and thirsty animals tore southward to Wolf Creek in a pell-mell run. After drinking, they came out on a prairie about a hundred and fifty yards from the creek, and stopped to rest. They had commenced lying down when Cook, from his camp on the creek above the herd, came within gunshot. He was not more than eighty steps away from the herd when he began shooting.

He shot a tremendously large bull first—the one he guessed to be the leader. Not half the buffaloes lying down rose at the report of the gun; but after Cook had accounted for three more buffalo in three shots some of the buffalo moved off toward the creek. Getting a good shot at the leader, Cook stopped him and the rest went no farther.

Cook realized now that he had what he had often heard talked about but never seen—a stand. Charlie

[6] John R. Cook, *The Border and the Buffalo* (Topeka, 1907).

Hart, he remembered, had given him some good pointers on the management of a stand—not to shoot fast enough to heat the gun barrel to over-expansion; always to try to hit the outside buffaloes; to shoot at any that started to walk off.

After he had killed twenty-five or more, the gunsmoke overhung him so that he crawled from under his pall and got even closer to the buffalo. He had shot a few more times, when he heard some one whistle behind him; it was his partner, Charlie Cook. "He was on all-fours, creeping up to me. He said: 'Go ahead; take it easy; I am coming with more cartridges.' He crawled right up to my side with my gun [John Cook was using a borrowed one] and an extra sack of ammunition for me, and a canteen of water. He asked if the gun was shooting all right. I told him 'Yes; but the barrel is pretty warm.' He told me to try my own gun a while and let his gun cool a little. We exchanged guns, and I commenced again."

He fired slowly and deliberately. Charlie Cook swabbed out the barrel of the used gun, and left the breech lock open to cool the barrel.

John Cook changed guns twice again. A shot from his own gun broke the leg of a big bull, who broke away; the rest of the herd followed him, and the "stand" was broken. Eighty-eight buffalo had been killed.

Colonel Dodge once counted one hundred and twelve carcasses within a semicircle: "all of which had been killed by one man from the same spot, and in less than three-quarters of an hour."

After the kill came the work of skinning the carcasses. A capable man could skin fifty buffaloes a day. The usual pay was about fifty dollars a month. Skinners were sometimes paid by the hide, as much as twenty-five or thirty cents each.

Some large outfits speeded up the work of removing the hides by using horses. The skinner split the hide from the head down to the tail, and loosened the hide from the legs, the head, and the tail. Ropes were then attached to the skin, and the tugs of the horse pulled the hide from the flesh. The hides were then taken to camp and pegged out. Small holes were cut through a hide around its outer edge, and pegs about six inches long, sharpened at one end and driven into the ground through the holes, stretched the hide to its proper shape. The strips of flesh that adhered were scraped off, and the hide left to dry. The last step was to fold and stack the dry skins. When the pile was about eight feet high, strings were cut from a green hide and tied through peg holes in each corner of the uppermost and the bottom hide, as tightly as the strings could be drawn. The pile was then

"HI, THE POOR BISON!"

From W. E. Webb (E. Hannaford, Chicago and Cincinnati, 1872). The original was entitled: "Five pictures for the consideration of Uncle Samuel, suggestive of a game law to protect his comb-horns, buttons, tallow, dried beef, tongues, robes, ivory black, bone-dust, hair, hides, etc.."

ready to be "boosted" upon the wagon and driven to a buyer.

In 1872 and 1873 the Atchison, Topeka and Santa Fe carried east about 424,000 buffalo robes and hides. The Kansas Pacific and the Union Pacific each carried as many—in all, about 1,250,000 buffalo skins were carried by the three western railroads. The Indians of all tribes within any distance of the great southern herd killed an immense number of buffalo—probably 350,000 for the two years. The farmers of eastern Kansas and Nebraska killed thousands of buffalo for meat. "Pretty much everybody" made a trip westward in the fall and brought back one or two wagonloads of buffalo meat. Very few skins were saved; the farmers didn't know how to tan them. In Wichita buffalo steaks, fine and tender, sold for one or two cents a pound.

In 1872 Colonel Dodge escorted three English gentlemen on a hunt in the Arkansas River valley; and in their enthusiasm the strangers "bagged more buffalo than would have supplied a brigade." From within a few miles of Fort Dodge, the colonel complained, his pleasure was frequently marred by the great numbers of buffalo, for they interfered with the more exciting pursuit of other game. In the fall of 1873 he went with two of the same English gentlemen over the same ground: "Where there were myriads of buffalo the year before, there were now myriads of carcasses. The air was foul with a sickening stench, and the vast plain, which only a short twelvemonth ago teemed with animal life, was a dead, solitary, putrid desert. We were obliged to travel southwest to the Cimmaron, a distance of nearly ninety miles, before we found a respectable herd. Even there we found the inevitable hunter." [7]

[7] R. I. Dodge, *Our Wild Indians* (Cincinnati, 1882).

CHAPTER IX

GENTLEMEN IN WASHINGTON

THE turbulent response of Congress to the demand of the West, voiced by Senator Douglas of Illinois, for a transwestern railroad, was the beginning of the move to edge out the Plains Indian from the attractive regions which he held in often-confirmed perpetuity. Mr. Manypenny, Commissioner of Indian Affairs, had the disagreeable duty of giving the Indians a powerful shove westward; and he did the best he could. When his negotiations were completed, he reminded Congress that by blends of persuasion and force tribes had been removed, step by step, from reservation to reservation, until now they could be pushed no farther; "on the ground they now occupy must the crisis be met, and their future determined." Mr. Manypenny was an honest fellow; but he lacked the imperial imagination.

The corruptions within the Bureau of Indian Affairs and in the army within the next ten years prevented any possible quieting of Indian unrest; and a special Committee on the Condition of the

Indian Tribes, beginning its work in 1865, reported two years later that the Indians should no longer be permitted to exist as roving tribes.

Yet in 1869 the Cheyennes and Arapahoes, and other Plains tribes in the heart of the buffalo range, were living in much the same way as their fathers thirty years before. They hunted the buffalo for food, for robes, and for lodges; they bartered robes to traders for eight or ten cups of sugar, or three or four cups of coffee. The squaws embroidered some of the robes with porcupine quills, and these brought as much as fifteen cups of sugar. And the braves occasionally killed a few white men.

Felix Brunot, Indian Commissioner, came to the Cheyennes and Arapahoes in the summer of 1869. He opened the council: "When there is much wood the camp-fires burn high and bright; when the wood is scarce the camp-fires burn low; when it is all gone the fire dies out. When the sun shines it is bright and warm; when it goes beyond the hills it does not die—it is bright and warm every day. The white man is like the sun. The Indian is like the camp-fire. The buffalo are getting scarcer every day. If you do not learn to live like the white man your nation will die out like the camp-fires." Medicine Arrow, the Cheyenne chief, answered that his tribe had been greatly molested by white men, but the Cheyennes were ready to make peace. And, a "lasting peace" having been negotiated, Medicine Arrow said that he would now like to trade for ammunition. . . .

Commissioner Parker pointed out to Congress in 1869: "Many good men, looking at the matter from a Christian point of view, will perhaps say that the poor Indian has been greatly wronged and ill treated; that this whole country was once his, of which he has been despoiled, and that he has been driven from place to place until he has hardly left to him a spot where to lay his head. This indeed may be philanthropic and humane, but the stern letter of the law admits of no such conclusion, and great injury has been done to the government in deluding this people into the belief of their being independent sovereignties, while they were at the same time recognized only as its dependents and wards." In 1871 the delusion was cleared away by an act that thereafter no Indian tribe within the territory of the United States should be recognized as a power entitled to make treaties with the United States. The act, while it speeded up the process of removal, did end a humiliating farce for both parties.

In the year that this brusque and unsentimental act was passed, a Cæsar with vision stepped from obscurity into the Secretaryship of the Interior. His name was Columbus Delano; and he bore the White

Man's Burden. The "bone and sinew of the nation," as their politicians loved to call them—the western farmers, whose fathers had been western farmers in Illinois, and whose grandfathers had been western farmers in Ohio or in Kentucky—had extended their definition of desirable lands to include practically the whole of the Great Plains; and Columbus Delano intended to see that they got what they wanted. For one thing, there were unpleasant currents of liberalism in Missouri and in other western states; and certainly, he may well have reasoned, the opening up of the buffalo range to the western farmers would not alienate the affections of western voters from the Grand Old Party.

His predecessor, J. D. Cox, had followed the policy of approving members of the Society of Friends for the Indian agencies; but Secretary Delano was done with such weaknesses. In his Annual Report for 1872 he pronounced sentence: "In our intercourse with the Indians it must always be borne in mind that we are the most powerful party. . . . We are assuming, and I think with propriety, that our civilization ought to take the place of their barbarous habits. We therefore claim the right to control the soil which they occupy, and we assume that it is our duty to coerce them, if necessary, into the adoption and practice of our habits and customs." There were, he estimated, somewhat over two hundred and forty thousand Indians in the West. The entire Indian population should be removed to the Indian Territory, releasing 93,692,731 acres of land for the "bone and sinew of the nation" to claim and to cultivate.

Columbus Delano had a pleasant plan of coercion. Buffalo hunters were already swarming into the range, held in theory by the Indians; if the Government should encourage them, or for that matter simply ignore them, the central fact of the Indian's mode of life would become a myth, and the tribes would have their choice of the Great Plains and starvation, or the Indian Territory and agriculture.

In June of 1871 Red Cloud, the Sioux chief, told a group of commissioners: "The Great Spirit raised both the white man and the Indian. I think he raised the Indian first. He raised me in this land and it belongs to me. The white man was raised over the waters, and his home is over there. Since they have crossed the sea, I have given them room. There are now white people all about me. I have but a small spot of land left. The Great Spirit told me to keep it. I went and told the Great Father so. [Red Cloud had been to Washington, and there had had the pleasure of meeting President Grant.] When I went to him I asked for no annuity goods; all I asked for was my lands—the little spot I have left." The Dakota Sioux that summer hunted in western Nebraska and Kansas, peacefully sharing the buffalo range with other parties from other tribes that in earlier years they would have warred with. There was a common enemy now.

The delegation of the Sioux that had seen Grant had also seen Columbus Delano. The-Man-that-Packs-the-Eagle had addressed the secretary, reminding him that the young men of the Great Father were making roads through and settling in the Indian country and driving off their game. He wanted to know if the Great Father intended to permit this to continue. Mr. Delano answered noncommittally.

In his Annual Report for 1873 the Secretary of the Interior mentioned that serious complaints were being made to his department relative to the presence, upon Indian reservations, of white men who went there solely to kill buffalo; and while he thought that something should, perhaps, be done about it, "I would not seriously regret the total disappearance of the buffalo from our western prairies, in its effect upon the Indians, regarding it rather as a means of hastening their sense of dependence upon the products of the soil and their own labors."

The agent at the Upper Arkansas Agency was in 1874 threatened with mob law by a prominent newspaper in southern Kansas for having removed a party of buffalo hunters from the reservation. He reported that "horse thieves, whiskey peddlers, and buffalo hunters" were bold and defiant.

An attempt was made to induce the Cheyennes to send their children to the agency school; but the agents found it impossible. Schools were well enough for Arapahoes, the Cheyennes said, but Cheyenne children did not have to go to school to learn to hunt buffalo; and as for trade education and agricultural education, the Cheyennes had no desire to live after the buffalo had become extinct.

A party of Cheyennes and Arapahoes visited President Grant in 1874. Their chief complaint was of the whiskey peddlers and buffalo hunters in their country; and the President promised them that these undesirables should certainly be kept out. The manner in which this promise was kept may help to explain the futile wars and the final extermination which the Cheyennes brought upon themselves.

In Congress there were—as there always are—a few men who believed that the progress of Empire should be attended with a little decency. The policy of starving the Indians into agrarianism, of killing off the buffalo as quickly and completely as possible, was resented by these men, who made themselves heard in behalf of the preservation of the buffalo and of the honor of the Government.

R. C. McCormick, of Arizona, made the first move to arrest the butchery. On the last day of March 1871, he introduced a bill providing "that, excepting for the purpose of using the meat for food or preserving the skin, it shall be unlawful for any person to kill the bison, or buffalo, found anywhere upon the public lands of the United States; and for the violation of this law the offender shall, upon conviction before any court of competent jurisdiction, be liable to a fine of $100 for each animal killed." It was ordered to be printed, and promptly became lost among other such wastepaper on Representatives' desks.

Senator Cornelius Cole, of California, in February of the next year asked that the Committee on Territories be directed to inquire into the desirability of an enactment for the preservation of the buffalo, elk, and other useful wild animals, against indiscriminate slaughter and extermination. The committee received, two days after, a bill written by Henry Wilson of Massachusetts to restrict the killing of buffalo upon the public lands; and refused to report it to the Senate.

McCormick, in April, again pressed his defense of "the finest wild animal in our hemisphere" before the House. He pointed out that prominent officers in the Army could not stomach the wantonness. Several of them had written to Henry

Bergh, president of the American Society for the Prevention of Cruelty to Animals, hoping for some civil agitation as a last resort. Major General Hazen had written: "The theory that the buffalo should be killed to deprive the Indians of food is a fallacy, as these people are becoming harmless under a rule of justice." Lieutenant Colonel Brackett added: "All the reports about fine sport and good shooting are mere gammon. It would be equally as good sport, and equally as dangerous, to ride into a herd of tame cattle and butcher them indiscriminately. The wholesale butchery of buffaloes upon the plains is as needless as it is cruel." McCormick presented a third letter written to Mr. Bergh, from one who had been thirteen years on the Plains as an Indian Agent and in the Army: "There is another strong reason, apart from cruelty, etc., which should compel Congress to take action; it is one of the greatest grievances the Indians have; and, to my personal knowledge, has frequently been their strongest incentive to declare war. Little Robe, the Cheyenne chief, who recently visited Washington, at one time remarked to me after I had censured him for allowing his young men to kill a white man's ox: 'Your people make big talk, and sometimes make war, if an Indian kills a white man's ox to keep his wife and children from starving; what do you think my people ought to say when they themselves see their cattle killed by your race when they are not hungry?' "

For the rest of 1872, and throughout the next year, while hunters were holding high jamboree in the Platte and Republican River country, and Columbus Delano, in his secretaryship, smirked with satisfaction as he envisaged a prairie clotted with rotting buffalo, the matter of preservation was not mentioned in Congress.

Early in 1874 Representative Fort of Illinois introduced a bill similar to those that had preceded it; and in March the Committee on Territories returned it to the House with the recommendation that it be passed.

The first section of the bill provided that it should be unlawful for any one not an Indian to kill, wound, or in any way destroy any female buffalo of any age, found at large within any Territory of the United States. The second section declared it unlawful for any such person to kill or wound any greater number of male buffaloes than were needed for food by that person, or more than could be used for the food of other persons, or for the market. Any person assisting in unlawful killing of the buffalo should also be held liable. For the second offense there was a possible penalty of thirty days' imprisonment.

Mr. McCormick recalled how he, with a hundred

other passengers, had been snowbound in a Kansas Pacific Railroad train, and that for some days the passengers had subsisted entirely upon the meat of the buffalo. He read an extract from a Santa Fe newspaper: "The buffalo slaughter, which has been going on the past few years on the plains, and which increases every year, is wantonly wicked, and should be stopped by the most stringent enactments and most vigilant enforcements of the law. Killing these noble animals for their hides simply, or to gratify the pleasure of some Russian duke or English lord, is a species of vandalism which cannot too quickly be checked. United States surveying parties report that there are two thousand hunters on the plains killing these animals for their hides. One party of sixteen hunters report having killed twenty-eight thousand buffaloes during the past summer. It seems to us there is quite as much reason why the Government should protect the buffalo as the Indians."

Representative Cox assumed the burden of the opposition. This delicate matter of the sexes, now: Mr. Cox understood that it was quite impossible for hunters to tell the sex of a running buffalo. (William T. Hornaday has commented, "I know of no greater affront that could be offered to the intelligence of a genuine buffalo hunter than to accuse him of not knowing enough to tell the sex

of a buffalo 'on the run' by its form alone.") And
the bill wasn't fair; it made an exception in favor
of the Indians: "Would it be in order to strike out
the clause excepting the Indians from the operation of this bill? The Secretary of the Interior has
already said that the civilization of the Indian is
impossible while the buffalo remains upon the
plains."

To which orthodoxy Representative Fort replied,
"I am not in favor of civilizing the Indian by starving him to death, by destroying the means which
God has given him for his support." And Representative Eldridge, concurring, said, "The argu-
ment, Mr. Speaker, is a disgrace to anybody who
makes it."

Mr. Eldridge had been in the West the previous
autumn; and had met several parties on their way
to the range to kill buffaloes for sport: "They were
men from abroad, foreigners, who had come to this
country to have the honor of saying that they had
killed a buffalo. I was told that they went to the
plains and shot down these animals, not even de-
siring to take their tongues or their pelts, and left
them to rot upon the plains. These same travelers,
these foreigners, who go out to kill the buffalo in
wanton sport, are also protected by our military
force. We not only allow them to come here and
kill the buffalo wantonly and wickedly, but at the

HUNTING WITH BOW AND ARROW

From George Catlin, *North American Indian Portfolio* (George Catlin, London, n. d.).

same time we afford them protection by our arms." And a colleague rushed into the discussion: "Not only that; but they are furnished horses by the army to go out and kill the buffalo."

Mr. Parker of Missouri announced that, in his judgment, the key to the solution of the Indian problem was to confine the Indians to as small a tract as possible, and to make it a necessity for them to labor and get their subsistence from the soil. He pointed out that, by a pleasant coincidence, the Secretary of the Interior entertained exactly the same opinion.

Others of the Secretariat's yes-men were heard from: one of them stated, "The bill is utterly worthless in point of fact. There is no law which human hands can write, there is no law which a Congress of men can enact, that will stay the appearance of these wild animals before civilization. They eat the grass. They trample upon the plains. They are as uncivilized as the Indian." [1]

The bill was passed. Sent to the Senate, there was very little discussion; the bill was ratified, and sent to the President for his signature. Ulysses S. Grant received it and put the document into a pigeonhole for its India ink to become a rich brown before it

[1] The documentary history of these attempts at legislation is as follows: H. R. 157, Forty-second Congress, First Session; S. 655, Forty-second Congress, Second Session; H. R. 921, Forty-third Congress, First Session.

was seen again. Or perhaps he touched the bill to his lamp, and lighted a cigar with it.

Colonel Herchmer, a commissioner of the Royal Northwest Mounted Police, once made the interesting charge—unanswered—that the United States Government sent out sharpshooters, and furnished them with Winchester rifles, to destroy the buffalo and thus to force the Sioux and other restless tribes to sue for peace and mercy. This, he thinks, was in revenge for the Custer massacre.

When old cattlemen meet and exchange recollections of their early trail-driving days, one of them will sometimes date his anecdote: "That was the year the Government began killing off the buffalo."

CHAPTER X

THE SOUTHERN RANGE: LAST YEARS

BY the spring of 1874 the hunters assembled at Dodge City were convinced that never again would the great herd of buffalo run that far north; and, their guns restless, they talked of the hunting country below the Cimmaron and about the Canadian River.

The terms of the Medicine Lodge Treaty had provided that white hunters should not cross the Arkansas River; the country to the south, as far as the Texas boundary, was proclaimed a "military district," "set apart for the exclusive use of the Cheyennes, Arapahoes, Kiowas, and Comanches, and such other bands as might be located there"; and troops occasionally patrolled the banks of the Arkansas. The menace to adventurers was, of course, not the troops but the Indians. Until after 1870 it was considered almost suicidal to violate the dead line. Some hunters took desperate chances to hunt pelts and furs south of the Arkansas, in winter, but they were very few, and some of them never returned. Curly Walker and Jack Pratte were two hunters who made the venture each year, each man for himself, with strong, light wagons and good horses. They always returned to Dodge City with loaded wagons, and here they traded with Bob Wright. But as long as the buffalo were plentiful north of the Arkansas, the dead line was generally respected by the hunters. Hunts on the Cimmaron, however, were common in 1873, and hunters feared that by the next spring the buffalo might have learned to cut their northern migration at the Canadian.

There was this objection to the migration of the hunters themselves: the long haul of their furs and robes from the Canadian range to a market at Dodge City. Robe-trader Myers solved that problem by deciding to take his outfit and stock of merchandise and move south with the hunters.

When the caravan moved out of Dodge City it included about fifty men, all mounted, and about thirty wagons. A party of friends was taking a pleasant excursion. In the party were veterans of the Civil War, reciting bloody recollections to tickle the appetite for buffalo killing. Near the night's camp fire two men would stretch and peg down a dry buffalo hide, on which the hunters would dance turn about or—for rich smutty effect—in couples. "There were always fiddlers in a crowd like ours," wrote Billy Dixon, one of the party, "perhaps an accordeon, and a dozen fellows who could play the French harp. . . . We heard nothing and cared nothing about politics." Another of the hunters was moved to poetry:

When the day's hunt is over, and all have had their dinners,
The hunter lights his pipe, to entertain the skinners;
He tells of the big bull that bravely met its fate;
Of the splendid line shot that settled its mate;
Of the cow, shot too low, of another, shot too high;
And of all the shots that missed he tells the reason why;
How the spike stood his ground, when all but him had fled,
And he refused to give it up until he filled him with lead;
How he traveled up the trail for five miles or more,
Leaving over forty victims weltering in their gore.
 . . . . . .
A tender-footed hunter is a great greenhorn,
And the poor old granger is an object of scorn,
But the worst deal of all is reserved for his buyers,
Who are swindlers and robbers and professional liars.

William Bent, the impresario of the old Santa Fe trade, had sent a party to build a trading post within the range of the Kiowas and Comanches. These tribes had droves of horses that might be traded for, and could supply the traders with "jerked beef." Near the south fork of the Canadian, in what is now Hutchinson County, Texas, the post was built. But the Comanches, leading a roving existence in the track of the buffalo, had rather shoot white men than trade with them. Hostilities compelled the abandonment of the station.

Here, at the ruins of the sun-baked walls, the buffalo hunters from Kansas took up headquarters. Two sod houses were built for storerooms; a stockade corral was put up; and another firm from Dodge City came down to compete with Myers for the trade. One Hanrahan built a saloon.

The spring was unusually late; and while the men waited for the buffalo they loitered about Adobe Walls, "joining in the fun that was rampant at that place. Our amusements were mostly card-playing, running horse-races, drinking whiskey and shooting at targets."

The great herd came at last, and the hunters broke up into outfits. The gunmen killed all they could, working their skinners furiously to keep up. It was deadly business, without sentiment. Several isolated parties were shot down by the Indians, and scalped. But the hunters had no intention of abandoning the range. The herds were at hand; prices were good; the hunters were in a fair way to make money. "Furthermore," commented Billy Dixon, "the buffaloes were becoming scarcer and scarcer each year, and it was expedient that we make hay while the sun shone. . . . After all, it was not unusual to hear of two or three buffalo-hunters being scalped each year."

As the weather became truly Texan, the doors of the sod houses were left open at night to catch such breezes as there were, and many of the men slept out of doors. There was no need of getting up until late in the morning.

But a great medicine man had become prominent among the Quahada Comanches. He had ascended to the abode of a Great Spirit high above the heaven of the white man's Father, and there he had learned to control the elements, to produce rain or cause a drought; from his stomach he could bring forth as many cartridges as the Indians needed; and his black magic could so influence the guns of the white men that they could not shoot Indians. The Comanches, now that their medicine man had made them invincible in battle, planned to kill the enemy tribe of the Tonkaways. But the commander of the Kiowa and Comanche Agency discovered the plan, and the Tonkaways were removed to the protection of Fort Griffin.

The Comanches then abandoned this scheme for a grander design. The pipe was carried to the Cheyennes and Arapahoes, the Kiowas, and the Apaches, and the Comanches asked them to aid in destroying the hunters, who were slaying the Indians' buffalo by thousands. The other tribes were eager; and the attack on Adobe Walls was planned. I-sa-tai, the inspired Comanche, had prepared his medicine carefully, and in consequence the doors of the houses would be open and the hunters would have been charmed into sleep. The Indians were to be daubed with war paint over which I-sa-tai had worked magic, and they would kill and scalp every buffalo hunter at the Walls without the loss of a brave.

On the night of June 26-27, 1874, there were twenty-eight men, and one woman—who had come with her husband from Dodge City to open a restaurant—at Adobe Walls. Twenty-five of them were sleeping in the buildings; two hunters and a Mexican bullwhacker were sleeping outside, in their wagons.

About three o'clock in the morning the men were awakened by a sudden crash: the ridgepole in James Hanrahan's saloon had cracked, and the roof threatened to give way. The work of propping up the roof lasted until almost dawn; the interruption had made the men too restless to sleep again, and they decided for an early start for the day's hunting. A man was sent to bring in the horses.

On the hills near Adobe Walls the Indians had been waiting for dawn. The medicine man was to be their chief in battle. He stood, naked except for a cap made of sage stems, to the right of the line, making his final invocations. About daylight he gave the call to charge. And Billy Ogg, before he reached the horses, discovered the long string of Indian braves swinging down upon Adobe Walls.

"Hundreds of warriors, the flower of the fighting men of the Southwestern Plains tribes, mounted upon their finest horses, armed with guns and lances, and carrying a heavy shield of thick buffalo hide, were coming like the wind. Over all was splashed the rich colors of red, vermilion, and ochre, on the bodies of the men, on the running horses. Scalps dangled from bridles, gorgeous warbonnets fluttered their plumes, bright feathers dangled from the tails and manes of the horses." But each one of the fourteen guns in Adobe Walls was loaded and waiting.

The three men outside the Walls could not be warned in time; they were quickly discovered and killed, and the Indians swarmed about the two houses and the saloon. Their magic would surely protect them; so they fought without fear, taking no care for their lives and charging directly to the doors of the buildings. As the defenders of Adobe Walls shot from the portholes, they placed the muzzles of their guns on the very faces of the savages.

For two hours the Indians made an incessant assault, battering the doors of one building partly open, but not effecting an entrance. Riderless horses dashed back and forth through the bombardment of guns, lances, and arrows.

"At one time there was a lull in the fight," Bob Wright related; "there was a young warrior, more daring and desperate than his fellows, mounted on a magnificent pony, decorated with a gaudy war-bonnet, and his other apparel equally as brilliant, who wanted, perhaps, to gain distinction for his bravery and become a great chief of his tribe, made a bold dash from among his companions toward the buildings. He rode with the speed of an eagle, and as straight as an arrow, for the side of the building where the port-holes were most numerous and danger greatest, succeeded in reaching them, and, leaping from his horse, pushed his six-shooter through a port-hole and emptied it, filling the room with smoke. He then attempted a retreat, but in a moment he was shot down; he staggered to his feet, but was again shot down, and, whilst lying on the ground, he deliberately drew another pistol from his belt and blew out his brains."

In the afternoon the Indians made another assault, but had to be content with carrying off some of their fallen. They left a field strewn with dead horses and dead Indians.[1] They had killed one buffalo hunter, and another had been killed when the hammer of his gun struck an obstruction and the accidental discharge tore into his head.

[1] Best accounts of the Battle of Adobe Walls are in: Billy Dixon, *The Life of Billy Dixon* (Oklahoma City, 1909); Mrs. Olive K. Dixon, *The Life of "Billy" Dixon* (Dallas, 1927); Robert M. Wright, *Dodge City the Cowboy Capital* (n. p. 1913). See also *House Executive Documents,* Vol. I, Forty-third Congress, Second Session.

Thirty-eight years later I-sa-tai, the medicine man, living at Fort Sill, avowed that the outcome of the battle of Adobe Walls was not the fault of his medicine; but that the morning after the Indians had started out some Cheyenne killed a skunk, and so shattered the force of his magic.

The hunters were escorted back to Dodge City, some ten days after the battle, by three companies of cavalry. General Miles was assigned to head an expedition against the Indian bands in the Adobe Walls district.

But the Government seemed slow in its preparations to some buffalo hunters, and they decided to run the risks of the country below the Canadian without waiting for General Miles to make the region safe for hunting parties. Emmanuel Dubbs and his friend Peters decided to go out as partners; they found two men willing to take chances at seventy-five dollars a month "and found," and prepared their supplies and ammunition.

They struck out for the Cimmaron, and continued south about thirty miles to a water hole on the prairie between Beaver and Wolf creeks. Here they found buffalo by the thousands; and they had not seen an Indian on the whole trip. Still, wary, they camped on the level flat as the safest place they could select, and took turns in standing night guard. In five days the skinners had two hundred hides pegged out to dry, and in a few more days the packs were in the wagons waiting to be moved. The camp had made ready for the retreat hurriedly, and the hides had been packed without folding and roughly tied with ropes. This carelessness cost the life of one of the buffalo hunters.

The loads kept slipping; and when the wagons came within a mile and a half of the little creek with cottonwood trees lining its banks, Peters rode off to cut some "boom poles" to be fastened across the packs.

His partner's anxiety grew as Peters' stay lengthened unaccountably, and Dubbs rode off toward the creek. He had not gone far when he came across a letter addressed to Peters that the high wind had tossed into a bush. Peters carried his letters—from a young lady who had made him promise that this was to be his last trip—in an oilcloth case in his inside vest pocket. That letter was ample testimony that the Indians had found Peters.

Dubbs and his two skinners threw off about half the hides from each wagon, to lighten the load. The party traveled slowly and carefully; each man kept his loaded gun by him. At one o'clock that night they made camp. The band of Indians that had killed Peters did not attack the camp, however; but when Dubbs pressed forward the next day he found a circle of twelve dead ponies. The Indians had discovered, and tried to surround, the camp of another buffalo hunter, Fred Singer; but the "Big Fifties" of the buffalo hunters had won another battle.[2]

Other hunters besides these had refused to wait for Miles. A cavalcade of twenty-eight men and fourteen wagons left Dodge City. They had to travel to the flats between the Canadian River and Wolf Creek before they found any large herds. When the Indians, always expected, finally made the attack the hunters, organized like a military machine, defeated them, and then carried the fight against the Indians, raiding the Indian camp and stealing the horses.

When General Miles led his expedition against the Comanches and their allies, buffalo hunters scouted for him. In the battle that followed the overtaking, the Indians were badly defeated. With the warring bands disposed of, the merchants organized their forces for the same systematic slaughter in the Indian Territory and in the Panhandle that had wiped away the buffaloes of the Platte and Republican valleys. On Sweet Water Creek, in the Panhandle, Rath and Wright established a large post carrying all kinds of hunters' supplies; and about the post the mushroom settlement of Sweetwater

---

[2] Emmanuel Dubbs, etc., *Pioneer Days in the Southwest* (Guthrie, 1909).

sprang up overnight—a dance-hall, two restaurants, three saloons—and hunting outfits were continually coming, selling, celebrating, going.

The Springer Ranch, about three miles south of the Canadian on the army trail between Fort Dodge and the Panhandle post, Fort Elliott, became a center for buffalo hunters. The ranch was built like a blockhouse, with a dry pit encircling it, and loop-holes in the thick walls.

Fort Griffin, and the Quinn brothers' post further south in the Panhandle, were each a rendezvous for buffalo hunters. Loganstein and Company of Leavenworth kept an agent at Fort Griffin with in-structions to buy all the buffalo hides offered for sale, to pay for them on the range, and to have them hauled to Fort Worth for shipment. Rath and Wright of Dodge City were the chief competitors of the Leavenworth company in the field. The Dodge City firm shipped to buyers in the eastern states; all of Loganstein's hides were shipped to Europe. The British army wanted to obtain hides because it was interested in replacing many of its leather accouterments with buffalo leather, more pliant and elastic than cowhide, and therefore pre-ferred for buffers.

Of the men themselves who were so busily killing off the southern herd, something must be said. "The great American buffalo hunters, fearless as a

Bayard, unsavory as a skunk!" Colonel Richard Irving Dodge hailed them.

Certainly there is an interesting time sequence

THE RARE OLD PLAINSMAN OF THE NOVELS

From W. E. Webb, *Buffalo Land* (E. Hannaford, Chicago and Cincinnati, 1872).

between the sudden break in the profits of buffalo hunting, when the southern herd had been practically exterminated, and the sudden increase, particularly about Jackson's Hole, Wyoming, but noticeably throughout the West, in the business of horse stealing.

In one of Jim McIntire's buffalo-hunting trips three of the boys decided to steal the horses from the Terrell brothers' ranch, ten miles away from Jim's camp. The Terrell brothers were the first settlers at Fort Worth, and good friends of Jim's; so McIntire warned the ranchmen, and fired the three would-be horse thieves. "I guess they changed their minds about the matter," McIntire says, "for they never showed up at Terrell's and we never heard of them afterwards. A few days later we received information that the Indians had killed three men in that vicinity, but none of the hunters ever took the trouble to look it up."

If any buffalo hunter had claimed to be a better man than Jim McIntire, he would probably have invited himself into a fight, and have deserved the knockdown. But Jim didn't mind admitting: "I have killed Comanche and Kiowa Indians by the score, and once I killed and skinned a squaw and made a purse of her breast, which I carried for nine years." Jim himself, incidentally, left buffalo hunting for the barkeep business. He opened a saloon at Fort Belknap, Texas, and found it easier to take the silver quarters and shinplasters over the bar from the buffalo hunters than to go out into the buffalo range himself. "They would all line up and drink round after round of frontier whiskey," McIntire recalled. "At this stage I would begin watering the whiskey, and gradually got it so weak that it would hardly be recognized as whiskey. I did this in order to keep them from getting too full. I would also manage to collect about twice for every round. One man would order the drinks and pay for the same, and then I would go to the other end of the bar and pick out another fellow, saying that the last round of drinks was on him.[3]

A party of buffalo hunters "on a toot" at Fort Wallace decided that they needed some virile entertainment. Some one mentioned Buffalo Joe, a hunter who had some days before killed his rival in the attentions of a widow. Good: Buffalo Joe would do nicely. And his fellow hunters found him and hung him. When the passenger train drew up in the morning, the body of Buffalo Joe was still swinging on a telephone pole beside the station.

A little above Pueblo the Arkansas River flows in a deep pass—the Royal Gorge—through the Rocky Mountains. It was possible to lay only one railroad through the ravine; but two roads, the Denver and Rio Grande and the Atchison, Topeka and Santa Fe, each planned to use it. In the spring of 1878 the struggle broke out into a war of hired gunmen. The Santa Fe came to Dodge City, the old headquarters of the buffalo hunters, for its fighters. The editor of the local newspaper announced his willing-

[3] James McIntire, *Early Days in Texas* (Kansas City, 1902).

ness to bet that the Dodge City crew would speedily clear the right of way of the Santa Fe "of all obstructions." And the local historian was soon able to add: "Which they did in short order."

General Sheridan once recommended to the Texas legislature that it give every buffalo hunter within its boundaries a medal emblematical of civilization's gratitude. If a particularly gangrenous medal had been announced for award to the best buffalo hunter, the judges would have been hard pressed for a choice.

Charlie Rath was one of the best, surely; but he devoted most of his time to buying. On the Canadian River in 1873, Rath shot one hundred and seven buffaloes in a single stand.

Frank Carver, who has given professional exhibitions of the sustained accuracy of his trigger-finger, is said to have killed over fifty-five hundred buffalo in his "best" year.

A hunter who noncommitally called himself "Kentuck" made ten thousand dollars from the hunt in less than a year. He had a camp on a small stream south of Fort Wallace, where he killed three thousand, seven hundred buffaloes. He was waiting for the herd when it began its northern migration, and never had to shift camp.

Sam Carr followed the game alone. It was no unusual matter for him to kill, skin, and bring into his camp thirty-five or forty buffalo hides in a day. To do that consistently a man had to be an expert marksman, to know how to keep the herd milling, and to be skilled and quick at skinning the animals.

There was only one white buffalo among the five million and more of the southern herd. It fell to the gun of Prairie Dog Dave, who sold the robe to Robert Wright for one thousand dollars.

By the close of the hunting season of 1875 the great southern herd had ceased to exist. A remnant of perhaps fifteen thousand roamed in frightened bands across the sagebrush area in "No Man's Land" and across the desolate Llano Estacado to the Pecos River. Charles Hart, in 1875, fitted out the first foray of the old hunters from Kansas into the Brazos and Pease River region. His outfit camped at a fresh spring near the Salt Fork of the Brazos, "in the midst of a vast sea of animals," to quote one of his skinners; but by the end of the year the vast sea had been reduced to scattered flecks of foam. A bull train of ten wagons that came into Fort Worth in 1876 carried five thousand skins.

"Nesters" passing through the buffalo country to find a homestead stopped at the hunters' camps to buy meat. If the homesteaders had whiskey to trade, their wagons would leave laden with a whole winter's supply of buffalo meat. A pioneer in the settlement of north Texas has written: "There was always some expedition on foot, it seemed to me, an expedition of some sort into the wilderness, undertaken oftener than not merely to satisfy the roving nature of these restless, unsettled people." There were thousands of turkeys and prairie chickens, and plenty of antelopes and buffaloes to furnish excuse for a westward excursion. In winter the people of the little settlements hunted the buffalo for meat, tallow, and hides. Only the hind quarters from the fat cows were taken on the wagons; and the hump and hump ribs were eaten in camp. The hides were not sold; they were used as windbreaks over cracks in the doors, and for beds.

Charles Norris, cowboy, remembers: "The last herd of buffalo I ever saw was in the Panhandle of Texas. I came on in the May of 1886; I was driving a bunch of horses from Coldwater to Buffalo Springs, saw the buffalo herd about three miles off." Morris did not have his gun with him then, so on his return from Buffalo Springs he went to the cowboy camp, and waited: it was pitched near the only water in the region, and he knew that in a day or two the herd would come to the water. "On the second day the whole herd appeared. Now I had a good chance to count them, and they were 186. They drank very heavily and played about like calves. A number of them amused themselves by jumping off a bluff into the water four feet below them, then running around to a low place to jump off again. As soon as we had seen all we wished, we fired." [4]

In the fall and winter of 1887 hunting parties attacked the only band of buffaloes left alive in the Southwest. Fifty-two were killed; ten skins entire, and the heads of all fifty-two, were preserved for mounting, and sold for as high as one hundred and fifteen dollars for the skin of a full-grown bull. About fifteen of the robes were sold for twenty dollars each, and the remaining lot was brought by the Hudson's Bay Company for three hundred and fifty dollars.

[4] E. T. Seton, "The American Bison or Buffalo," *Scribner's Magazine*, XL.

CHAPTER XI

CARRION

WHILE the western country from the Platte to the Republican was being stippled with the carcasses of buffalo, the northern herd was battered unremittingly for the robes—sixty thousand, to twice that number—that annually were carried away by the steamboats on the Yellowstone and the Missouri.

There were many small traders in the foothills of the Rockies; but T. C. Power and I. G. Baker, both at Fort Benton, controlled the bulk of the robe trade. They had their own hunters, who made raids thrice weekly upon the buffalo herds; and they obtained many robes from the Indians. Competing traders had forced the price upward; Indians now received anything from a jug of whiskey to six dollars for a robe. From 1874 to 1877 there were annually shipped from Fort Benton eighty thousand to one hundred thousand buffalo robes; about thirty thousand mountain wolf skins; one hundred and fifty tons of antelope skins, besides some beaver, mink, and otter. Baker could remember a ride from

Sun River to Milk River, and thence to Fort Benton, about two hundred and ten miles: during the whole journey he was constantly surrounded by buffaloes, and never for a moment out of sight of them. This was the great northern herd, to which the professional buffalo hunters were to come when western Kansas and the Panhandle were desolate.

The buffaloes in the great Canadian plain between the Eagle Hills and the South Saskatchewan were better protected than the herds in the United States, by the remoteness of the "great motionless ocean" on which they fed; but around the wide circle of the prairie region were some fifteen thousand Indians and half-breeds preying upon scattered bands of buffalo. Twelve thousand buffaloes fell annually to the Blackfoot tribes alone, and many robes were sent east from Red River posts. The supply rooms in the posts of the Hudson's Bay Company were filled with many thousand bags of pemmican.

The kill by Indians was increasingly large. With the high mortality of treaties-in-perpetuity, the Government had found opportunity to crowd other tribes into the Sioux and Blackfoot hunting grounds. Intertribal hostilities flamed as rival hunting parties exploited the same restricted range.

The treaty of 1868 to secure perpetual peace and amity with the Ogallalas and Brules, in the Dakota

Territory, had provided that these Indians could hunt the buffalo "on any lands north of the North Platte, and on the Republican Fork of the Smoky Hill River, so long as the buffalo may range thereon in such numbers as to justify the chase." But the Indian agent assigned to them—who was also an army captain—informed them that in view of the exploitation of that hunting range by other, hostile tribes, that he could not permit his own charges to join the chase. In making his annual report the agent had a touch of conscience: "This loss of buffalo makes them very poor, having been accustomed to rely upon that game as a means of wealth, the robes taking the place of clothing, the sale of them providing them with the necessities and luxuries of their lives. In this connection I would respectfully urge that more annuity goods be forwarded to them."

In 1873 a commission was sent to confer with the bands of Northern Sioux, with a "proposition for the relinquishment" of their "unneeded territory." Chief Red Cloud and his band refused; "but"—to quote the commission—"on being told that the right would be taken from them," they agreed to the cession of much of their hunting privileges.

Prospectors and miners were invading the Crow reservation south of the Yellowstone; and there were hints that the Northern Pacific Railroad would

A HERD OF SURVIVORS IN WYOMING

Photographed by Dr. Joseph K. Dixon, by permission of the Department of the Interior; copyright, 1913, by Rodman Wanamaker.

prefer to lay its roadbed through this reservation. Accordingly the Board of Indian Commissioners called a grand council of the Crows. Felix Brunot, the chairman, persuaded them to take a new reservation, half as large, in the Judith basin south of the Missouri: "I know what is good for the Indians, and I want you to know it, too. I have been on the Platte, and on Wind River, and on the Missouri, and away to the ocean, and what do I see? You do not see it, but I do. I see the white man's towns coming further and further; they are almost here. A few years ago, where these towns were, there were buffalo. The buffalo used to be on the Platte, as they are now on the Big Horn and Powder River. They are all gone now. Why are they so plenty up here? They have been driven from there and have come up here. The Sioux cannot find any buffalo on the Platte, so they come up north to hunt them. If the Crows went to the Platte and the Republican, they would not find any buffalo there. They have come up here. And when they are killed off here, they will be all gone everywhere. Buffalo are the Indians' bread, but they are going away, and soon will all be gone. . . ."

Each of the Crow chiefs asked that they might be permitted to eat buffalo for a long time, to which the commissioners responded "Yes," and the Indians shook hands with them.

In 1875 the Secretary of the Interior reported to Congress on a little matter of finances connected with another Indian treaty. A commission in May of that year had assured the Sioux that they would be recompensed for giving up certain hunting grounds—a recompense promised in the treaty of 1868. In October Secretary Chandler wrote: "Attention is invited to the condition upon which the Sioux relinquished the right to hunt in Nebraska, namely, that in addition to the $25,000 heretofore appropriated, the Department agree to recommend the further appropriation of a like amount. While presenting the recommendation, however, I deem it my duty to state that under the terms of the treaty of 1868 that right probably no longer existed at the time the treaty was made, it having expired by the terms of the treaty itself. That treaty reserved to the Sioux 'the right to hunt . . . (on the Nebraska land) as long as the buffalo may range thereon in such numbers as to justify the chase.' It is the concurrent testimony of army officers and white settlers familiar with the section of country referred to as a hunting-ground, that the buffalo no longer range thereon 'in such numbers as to justify the chase.' "

In January of the next year the Indian agents at Spotted Tail and Red Cloud reported that the supplies of beef and flour for their Sioux charges would be exhausted by the first of March. Congress passed a deficiency bill appropriating $150,000 for the relief of the Sioux—on the first of April. Supplies did not arrive until summer. Such conditions, the apparent purpose of the Government to abandon them to starvation, naturally induced the best of the Sioux to go north to join the band of Sitting Bull. For several years a camp of Sioux on the Yellowstone River had been gradually gaining in adherents. They were Sitting Bull's band, the non-treaty Sioux; they lived on the buffalo—without permission from Washington. An Indian agent reported of them: "They consist of representatives from all the bands, who have rallied round one who claims never to have been a party to any treaty with the United States . . . a paradise of those who, tired of Government beef and restless under agency restraint, were venturesome enough to resort again to their old life by the chase . . . headquarters in the center of the buffalo country, surrounded by abundance of game."

The building of the Northern Pacific had been begun in 1870; it crawled through the Indian lands in Dakota Territory, and by 1876 the rails had reached the Missouri River. Here, at Bismarck, it received the buffalo robes that came down the Missouri and the Yellowstone. The invasion of the railroad, and the slaughter of the buffalo herds, were the grievances that brought Sitting Bull his warriors. The massacre of General Custer's men on the Little Big Horn, and the many other tragedies of the Sioux War of 1876 and 1877, figure as another entry in blood and money toward the cost of Columbus Delano's policy.

In the spring of 1879 the professional hunters that had hounded the southern herd for eight years discovered, dazed and almost unbelieving, that only a few thousand buffaloes remained—not enough to support the gunmen another season. In this year and the next these old hunters came into the northern buffalo range. At the season when the buffalo were in the Yellowstone country, fires— incendiary or natural—burned the grasses to the north of the herd, and thus hindered any migration into Canada, where the hunters could not follow.

The great triangle bounded by the Missouri, the Yellowstone, and the Musselshell was a favorite hunting ground of the professionals. The herds ranged from Dakota to well toward the watershed of the Rockies; and hunters' camps lined the Missouri, the Yellowstone, and their tributaries. By 1882 there were over five thousand hunters and skinners—to say nothing of Indians—in the northern range. The buffaloes were blocked from water; and a chain of sentinel camps backed against the

Canadian border let very few buffaloes escape into British territory.

Almost the entire southern half of Dakota Territory had been despoiled of buffalo fifteen years before, by the crowding of the Mississippi Sioux from Minnesota into the hunting grounds of the Missouri Sioux, the Pawnees, and the Omahas. Robe traders were active among the Indians, and the slaughter for food and robes had driven the surviving buffaloes into the north and west, where they joined with the great northern herd. The Indians had, of necessity, taken to farming, and lived squalidly and precariously, sowing, fighting grasshoppers, harvesting slim crops, receiving desultory doles of food and goods from the agencies, occasionally making hunting trips north after elk. Early in the fall of 1880, almost incredible rumors came to these Indians that the buffalo were coming back.

The cordon of the professional hunters, closing in upon the buffaloes from the north and south, sagged in the east. Migrations were from north to south, and back; the instinct of the buffalo was to run against the wind, and certainly there was little east wind in Montana. But in the frenzy of the incessant hunt the inherited characteristics of the buffalo were worthless and forgotten; and the buffalo turned to the east. It was a blind alley; but there was nowhere else to go.

The Dakota Sioux at the Cheyenne River Agency set out to find the buffalo—a cavalcade of sixty hunters, forty women, three hundred horses, and an unnumbered horde of dogs. There was one white man who went with them, Thomas L. Riggs, missionary to the Dakotas; his description is the only record of the last hunt of the tribe.[1]

One day a young man found what appeared to be the trail of a buffalo, half hidden by the drifting snow, and the whole camp was enjoined against firing a gun, for fear of frightening away the buffalo. The next day other buffalo trails were seen, and there was talk of sending runners ahead to locate the herd—if there was a herd. Two young men were selected for the scouting. Each, with hands rested palm down on the earth, received his instructions and made silent pledges. The earth was the mother of all things; and this prayer was offered lest the mother earth give alarm to the buffalo and carry to their ears rumblings that would reveal the approach of men.

These scouts, Riggs learned, would bear an honorable name if they returned with glad messages. "What do you call them when they have no message?" he asked. "We shall not see them at all if they have nothing to tell. They will not come

[1] Thomas L. Riggs, "The Last Buffalo Hunt," *Independent*, LXIII.

back till after dark, and then even the dogs of their own tents will not know them."

Just after sunset of the next day—an anxiously dull day for the camp—the runners came into view. The Indians gathered, facing them; each man brushed aside the snow before him and kneeled. The runners came straight to the camp crier. "The crier lighted a pipe, took a whiff himself, and after reverently touching the earth with the bowl and lifting the stem to heaven above, he presented it to the leader and said: 'You who are no longer children—grown up amidst the hills and valleys— tell me, I pray, if you have seen anything of prowling dog or flying bird and feeding animal beyond the hills from whence you came; tell me and make me glad.' The runner having received the pipe and in turn offering it to the earth and sky, takes a mouthful or two of smoke, and passing the pipe to his comrade, answers, 'Yes.' The expectant crowd gives voice to a shrill cry of exultation: 'Hai—i Hai—i!' "

The hunters started before dawn, mounted on pack horses and leading their running horses through the snowdrifts. These running horses had been let loose all the way out, and at every opportunity had been fed shavings of the inner bark and the twigs of young cottonwood trees: these were the horses on which the hunters depended for the chase. It was a cold, numbing morning—the day before Christmas.

Soon after daybreak some buffaloes were seen—not many, but the Indians were tired of venison, porcupine, skunk, and badger meat, and decided to run these buffalo.

Each man changed mounts, taking his running horse. The dog soldiers guided the party through a little valley that was the approach of the hunters. The signal for the run was given; the horses clambered up to the level ground where the buffalo were huddled together; and the hunt was on—a scramble of animals and men on the ice sheet beneath the snow, a confusion of wounded, floundering buffalo and eager, struggling horses and hunters. Only one buffalo escaped; and the party packed back to camp the meat from fifty carcasses. "The dogs that came from home lean and scrawny grew sleek and fat." Two thousand robes and much buffalo meat were taken back to the Cheyenne River Agency when the winter's hunt was over. In the spring the Dakota Indians were back in their fields; and no rumors ever led them west again.

In Montana at about the same time "Coquina," the star contributor of the *American Field,* was enjoying a buffalo hunt of a very different kind.[2]

[2] George O. Shields, *Hunting in the Great West* (New York, n. d.).

His fondest dream, he said, had been to hunt the buffalo in its native range, to see the antelope, the elk, and the coyote roaming at will in the uncurbed beauty of nature; and he came out to have a good time.

Crossing the Minnesota lake region on the Union Pacific, the literary hunter—George O. Shields—noticed the numerous flocks of ducks. The conductor told him that hunters commonly stood in the door of the baggage car and fired into the flocks as the train skirted past the shores.

Shields and his party went to Camp McIntosh, on Beaver Creek; the major in charge received them cordially, and announced himself glad to furnish an army escort and a wagon team or two to the sportsmen. At the major's mess tent for supper they had venison steak, antelope steak, broiled buffalo tenderloin, Saratoga potatoes, baked sweet potatoes, tomatoes, corn, other vegetables, fruits, pastry, and various beverages.

Once on the hunt, the next day, they shot into several small bands of buffalo; and that night the major's orderly and a half-breed scout, who had traveled in advance of the party, reported that they had seen the main northern herd, of at least two hundred thousand buffaloes, only twelve miles distant. That was something to dream about! And "Coquina" dropped a tear at the thought that the constant slaughter by hide hunters—"a burning shame and a disgrace to any civilized citizen"—would within five years wear this great herd to a fugitive shred. Congress should pass a law to prohibit this slaughter, he thought, and went to sleep.

In the morning he was zestful for the kill, and found and shot two old bulls before breakfast.

Into the Cabin Creek bad lands the party followed the buffaloes. Whenever they saw a herd they dismounted, and threw pot shots into the herd from an elbow rest. They stampeded one herd that plunged over a seventy-foot precipice and became a writhing, surging mass six to ten deep. The hunt was "a most pleasant and successful one in every respect, barring the weather of the last two days" to Mr. Shields. Sixty-four buffaloes, several antelopes and deer and some small game were killed. And Mr. Shields advised his readers, in the *American Field,* that those who would like to kill buffaloes had better hurry into the range while the getting was good.

Dickinson, located immediately east of the bad lands, became the main outfitting and shipping point for the buffalo hunters. Wagon trains unloaded vast piles of green hides for shipment. The Indian Agent at Standing Rock, to the southwest of Dickinson, was ready to extend every hospitality

A BIG KILL

From George Catlin, *North American Indian Portfolio* (George Catlin, London, n. d.).

to the buffalo butchers, and engaged the Sioux warriors to hasten their own humiliation by joining in the hunt and disposing of the hides they took to the professional hunters. In June of 1882 he promoted one debauch in which five thousand buffaloes were killed in two days.

The improved Sharp's rifles had telescopic sights, and a hunter on a good point of vantage could keep a distant herd milling indefinitely simply by picking off any bulls seeking to lead the herd away—could shoot with scarcely the possibility of a miss until his rifle became overheated. Hides were worth more now—two dollars to three-fifty; and there was not so much of the criminal waste that characterized the southern hunt. Every hundred hides carried to market, it has been estimated, represented not more than one hundred and ten dead buffaloes. In Kansas ten years before that many hides would have represented at least two hundred buffaloes. Much of the meat of these northern buffaloes was saved and marketed.

Joseph Ullman, the New York furrier, gave William T. Hornaday, investigating on behalf of the National Museum, these figures:

"In 1881 we handled about 14,000 hides, average cost about $3.50, and 12,000 robes, average cost about $7.50.

"In 1882 we purchased between 35,000 and

40,000 hides, at an average cost of about $3.50, and about 10,000 robes, at an average cost of $8.50.

"In 1883 we purchased from 6,000 to 7,000 hides and about 1,500 to 2,000 robes at a slight advance in price."

The Messrs. Moskowitz, furriers of New York and Chicago, purchased 35,000 robes and 4,500 hides in 1880; and 23,350 robes and 26,600 hides in 1881, at a total cost for these two years of over $430,000. In 1882 and 1883, buying as many robes and hides as they could, and paying higher prices, the sum of their payments for robes and hides was under $157,000.

There were many other furriers in Chicago and New York who bid for buffalo skins. In the British possessions, the buffalo-robe business was practically the monopoly of the Hudson's Bay Company.

Deep snows and hard winters in 1881 and 1882 gave the *coup de grâce* to the buffaloes that broke through the line of pot-hunters at the Canadian border and escaped the northern Indians.

At the beginning of the winter of 1882-83 the great herd, containing now about seventy-five thousand buffalo, was in the region about the Yellowstone. Fear overcame instinct, and the buffalo moved northward in one body; but it never reached the Canadian border. If it had escaped the professionals, it would probably have been destroyed by the Cree and Blackfeet Indians in Canada, half starved because only poor, lean buffalo had been found on their Canadian range after the vicious winters of the two previous years. The only vestige of the great herd that remained was a band of about two hundred that found shelter in the confusion of ravines and creek bottoms in the bad lands west of the Musselshell, and a band of about seventy-five that fled to the rough land above the source of Big Dry Creek, a tributary of the Missouri.

In the southeast a herd of about ten thousand head was ranging, at the beginning of the hunting season of 1883, about halfway between the Black Hills and Bismarck. The hunters speedily killed almost nine thousand of them. In October of 1883, when about eleven hundred of this herd remained, Sitting Bull and his band of nearly one thousand warriors arrived at the range. The white hunters joined them in one final orgy; and within two days the entire herd was annihilated.

And in the winter of 1883 the buffalo butchers outfitted as usual. They hired their skinners, they stocked their wagons with ammunition and provisions, and set out for the buffalo range. The buffaloes seemed to be farther west this year; and the hunters guided their wagons through the carrion of last season's hunts, toward the Rockies. But there were no buffalo. North there were none, only here and there a lone old bull. The buffalo butchers simply could not believe in this destitution, and they staggered into failure and bankruptcy.

In the spring of 1884, a robe buyer, one J. N. Davis of Minneapolis, collected enough robes at Dickinson to make a scant carload. It was the only such carload that went east that year; and the last shipment of buffalo robes on the Northern Pacific Railroad.

CHAPTER XII

SURVIVAL

THE flesh and tissues of the buffalo carcasses disintegrated, leaving white, bare skeletons. Homesteaders who came into the West with only an old wagon and older horses, several children, and a few dogs, got a start in their new existence by collecting the buffalo bones.[1] In the lean years of the seventies when the hot winds made tinder of the crops, the settlers drove their wagons into the unclaimed prairie and gathered up buffalo bones and horns to take to the nearest railroad station.

Springtime outran the furrowings of raw sod;
There must be bread; in August the bonepickers
Go harvesting the prairie, dragging out—
Rich roof for the hundred-legs and scurrying beetles—
From the fingers of the grass and spiderweb
Long curving rib and a broad white shoulder-blade.

[1] Hamlin Russell, "The Story of the Buffalo" (*Harper's Monthly,* LXXXVI); Joseph B. Thoburn, *A Standard History of Oklahoma,* Vol. II (Chicago and New York, 1916); Robert I. Garden, *History of Scott Township,* Iowa (Oskaloosa, Iowa, n. d.). And let me here acknowledge the courtesy of Edwin Ford Piper, from whose poem "Dry Bones" I have borrowed a verse.

Fertilizing plants bought the bones to make into phosphates; sugar refineries bought the bones for carbon.

The gathering of buffalo bones became a regular industry as early as 1872, when the farmers followed the buffalo butchers into the range that had just been devastated; over a million pounds were shipped on the Santa Fe that year. In 1873 the Santa Fe carried over two million, seven hundred and forty thousand pounds of buffalo bones, and in 1874 —when the hunters had followed the buffalo below the Cimmaron, and the "fool hoe-men" (as the cowboys called them) were rapidly claiming Kansas for their own—the railroad shipped east almost seven million tons of buffalo bones. "Buffalo bones are legal tender in Dodge City" is a common newspaper quip in 1874. There were great stacks, hundreds of tons of bones, piled up beside the Santa Fe track. Bone stacks towered above the box cars; and often there were not enough cars to move them. John Cook saw "a rick of buffalo bones, on the Santa Fe railroad right of way, and twenty miles ahead of the track from Granada, Colorado, piled twelve feet high, nearly that wide at the base, and one-half mile long. Seven, eight, nine, and ten dollars a ton was realized on them."

Although the railroad was a long way from the buffalo range of Indian Territory, hundreds of wagon loads of bones were hauled from this Oklahoma country to Wichita or some other railroad station. Freighters returning with empty wagons after having taken their goods to the military posts or the Indian agencies, stopped in the Cimmaron valley, or near the Salt Fork, and loaded their wagons with buffalo bones. Scott Cummins, the Pilgrim Bard of Oklahoma, did his best to immortalize the bone freighter; he scratched with a bullet upon the bleached shoulder blade of a buffalo six pathetic verses entitled "The Song of the Bone Pilgrim."

A freight train from Abilene, Texas, to New Orleans, in 1880, with a full complement of box cars, carried nothing but buffalo bones. A fancy price was paid; the news spread; and bone haulers flocked into the Panhandle and eastern Colorado. Prairie fires had destroyed millions of pounds before the salvagers came; but the business lasted for nearly two years. The markets were glutted; but the average price for a ton of buffalo bones delivered at the railway station did not fall below four dollars.

Indians whose game was gone, and whose destitution the Government was only slowly relieving, collected the bones, got for them whatever the teamsters, commission men, brokers, railroad companies, and refineries left, and made a living—in a way.

By the end of the buffalo-hunting carnival in the

north, the Northern Pacific Railroad had been built across the buffalo range, and the business of collecting bones throve for a few years.

Julian Ralph and a friend were traveling westward on the Canadian Pacific in 1888. "As we journeyed on we found that the bison's remains had been made the basis of a thriving business. At the outset we saw a few bison bones dotting the grass in white specks here and there, and soon we met great trains, each of many box cars, laden with nothing but these weather-whitened relics. Presently we came to stations where, beside the tracks, mounds of these bones were heaped up and rude men were swelling the heaps with wagon loads garnered far from the railroad, for a great business has grown up in collecting these trophies. For years the business of carting them away has gone on."

In the spring of 1886 the directors of the National Museum at Washington decided to exhibit a mounted group of buffalo, "a small square patch from the wildest part of the wild West." But the Museum had almost no presentable specimens. The chief taxidermist discovered, after extensive correspondence, thàt the destruction of all the large herds, outside the remote, snowbound range in northern Canada, was already accomplished. The taxidermist was William T. Hornaday. Later a man in New Hampshire and another in Oklahoma were to render timely, vital service in the preservation of the buffalo; but the pioneer labor and inspiration of the taxidermist in Washington makes the rescue of the buffalo from extermination seem almost a personal achievement.

Hornaday's correspondence determined that there was a small band of six or eight wild buffaloes in southwestern Dakota—too few to justify the search —about two hundred buffalo in scattered bands in the Texas Panhandle—too difficult to reach, or hunters would already have killed them—and some stray buffalo about Big Dry Creek, Montana. Hornaday's expedition went into Montana, into the bad lands north of the Yellowstone.

It was a treeless country, specked with sage brush. Prairie dogs, rabbits, a few antelope . . . at last, buffalo. Three buffaloes were seen, two of them killed; and cowboys confirmed the existence of a band of thirty-five buffalo. But summer was already advanced, and the buffalo had lost their heavy pelage. Hornaday returned in the fall, when the buffalo would be more handsome.

In mid-October the bison were discovered. "We left the rugged butte region behind us, and entered a tract of country quite unlike anything we had found before. It was composed of a succession of rolling hills and deep hollows, smooth enough on the surface, to all appearances, but like a desert of sand hills to traverse. The dry soil was loose and crumbly, like loose ashes, and the hoofs of our horses sank into it half-way to the fet-locks at every step. But there was another feature which was still worse. The whole surface of the ground was cracked and seamed with a perfect network of great cracks, into which our horses stepped every yard or so, and sank down still farther, with many a tiresome wrench of the joints. It was terrible ground to go over. To make it as bad as possible, a thick growth of sage-brush or else greasewood was everywhere present for the horses to struggle through." It was such barren, tortuous country that had offered the remnant of the buffalo herd its only security.

Several weeks of searching passed, with stray buffalo occasionally discovered and shot, before the party had secured its twentieth skin. Nearly every full-grown bull which was killed carried several old bullets in its body. In December the hunt was ended; and fifteen months later a group of six buffalo snuffed at clumps of wax bunch grass, or bent to drink from a tranquil, glass pool, in the south hall of the National Museum.

Mr. Hornaday's report to the Smithsonian Institution in explanation of the expedition was the first careful history of the butchery that had dirtied the West, and became the textbook of those men who succeeded, ultimately, in making the American Government understand somewhat its obligations to the American scene. Sentimentalism? Of course: the surviving buffalo, behind their fences, are useless bulks, almost Pleistocene in their relation to the factory that made this barbed wire they scratch against. But a nation which should pretend it had no frontier phases in its geography or its culture would be a little insane. The conservation of the buffalo is, simply, a matter of good manners.

In the far north, in the quadrangle limited by the Peace River, Slave River, the Great Slave Lake, and the Caribou Mountains, a herd of buffalo had lived and bred, almost untouched by the hectic massacre. Wild hay and native grasses were in profusion; there were salt springs; the sand hills made excellent wallowing grounds. The country was too rigorous for white men; and the Indians of the region lived chiefly on fish, easier to get than buffalo.or moose. At the beginning of 1889 there must have been six hundred buffalo in this herd; and there were not as many as ninety wild buffalo throughout the Western States. The Dominion Government placed a permanent closed season on these buffalo, and entrusted the Northwest Mounted Police with their protection. By an Order-in-Council in 1922, ten thousand, five hundred square miles of the Slave River district, embracing the buffalo range, were set aside for all time; and experienced rangers in cabins throughout the district guard the pledge of Canada.[2]

The interest of the Canadian Government in the buffalo had begun in 1897, when a private gentleman presented three buffalo to the Rocky Mountains Park. In a generous enclosure at Banff, these buffalo (and one other, the gift of Lord Strathcoma in 1898) so multiplied under close attention and careful crossing that twelve years later the herd numbered over a hundred buffalo.

In 1907 the Dominion honored itself with a profoundly generous gesture: the purchase of Michael Pablo's herd of six hundred buffalo.

A half-breed Indian, Walking Coyote, in about 1880 had driven a band of thirty buffalo from Alberta into the Flathead Indian reservation in Montana. Another half-breed, Pablo, bought the herd for two thousand dollars, and protected his property well. When the Department of the Interior threatened him with the loss of his buffalo range, he approached the Canadian Government, first with an attempt to secure grazing land in Alberta, finally with an offer to sell the entire herd. Howard Douglas, Commissioner of Dominion Parks, made the bid of two hundred dollars a head. The Wainright

[2] American Bison Society, *Fourth Annual Report*; F. H. Kitto, "The American Bison in Canada" (*Geographical Journal*, LXIII); Newton McTavish, "The Last Great Roundup" (*Canadian Magazine*, XXXIII).

Buffalo Park was created to house this herd, and its hundred and sixty-two square miles enclosed with a steel fence.

The first four hundred of Pablo's herd were corraled and transported easily enough; but the remaining three hundred had to be "rounded up." Scouts were sent out to locate the scattered bands; miles of fenced runway were built; booms were laid in the Pend d'Oreille to prevent escape upstream. Halfbreed cowboy riders of the Montana hills mustered the buffalo into a corral; and in ponderous crates the animals were hauled, caravan style, to the nearest railroad station, thirty-five miles away.

In the United States Charles J. Jones, in Kansas, had a private herd of buffalo, and was occupied with attempts to cross the deposed monarch of the plains with the domestic cow, and make a work animal of him. Major Gordon W. Lillie at Pawnee, Charles J. Goodnight in the Panhandle, and "Scotty" Philip at Fort Pierre had private herds grazing on large ranches. But the movement to interest the American Government, to insure the permanence of the preservation, was not begun until 1904.[3]

In the summer of that year appeared the first

[3] The occasional *Reports* of the American Bison Society are indispensable in tracing the steps toward the preservation of the buffalo. Ernest H. Baynes, "In the Name of the American Bison" (*Harper's Weekly*, L), and Gordon W. Lillie, "Restoring the Bison to the

appeals of Ernest Harold Baynes for the buffalo, a series of articles in the Boston *Transcript*. His circle of influence grew until it reached the presidential chair. On December 8, 1905, fourteen men met to organize the American Bison Society. Hornaday was its president, Baynes its secretary, and Theodore Roosevelt its honorary president.

In the next two years Baynes gave lectures; wrote magazine articles ("This is literally the last call," he sounded in *Harper's Weekly*); induced others to write articles; reared buffalo calves by hand; broke two young buffaloes to harness, drove them in a gig, and at an agricultural fair raced to victory over a gig drawn by a domestic steer; and finally revived the old dream of making fabrics of the buffalo wool.

Meanwhile, in Oklahoma, another enthusiasm was afire. As Major Lillie, in a personal letter, recounts its beginning: "In about 1904 I saw an A. P. dispatch stating there was a carload of pure blood buffalo to be killed in Omaha and sold for Christmas dinners—I had seen the buffalo diminish to a mere handful—and felt that unless something was done to protect the few remaining that there was great danger of the buffalo becoming extinct. So I at once set out to protect and preserve the few re-

Western Plains" (*Cosmopolitan*, XXXIX), are good examples of the propaganda literature of 1905 and 1906.

maining. In 1906 I went to Washington and introduced through our Congressman, Hon. B. S. McGuire, the bill which gave us the buffalo preserve near Fort Sill, Oklahoma, that now numbers about one thousand head of as fine buffalo as are in existence."

Spurred by the lobbying of the American Bison Society, and belatedly aroused by the sale of the Pablo herd to Canada, the Government in 1908 established a national bison range of twelve thousand, five hundred acres in the Flathead Reservation, Montana; and the American Bison Society undertook to stock the range.

Ten thousand dollars must be raised for purchasing the nucleus of the herd; and the Society rose to its task. Gentlemen in New York contributed over one-half the amount; two thousand, three hundred dollars came from Massachusetts. The buffalo butchery had been its bloodiest in Kansas. Now Kansans pretended that their back yard was immaculate, and contributed not a cent.

By 1924 the Pablo herd in the Wainright Park had increased to five thousand, as many as the natural forage could support, and the Canadian Government has since moved the animal surplus to the Slave River Park. By 1925 the herd in the Yellowstone Park had become so large that the Government authorized the killing of a certain number.

In 1926 there were 4,376 buffaloes in the United States, and 11,957 in Canada.

And it is only thirty years ago that a band of Indians, in the spring, saddled their ponies and rode away—"as of old, but in silence and sadness."

"Where are you bound?" some white man asks; and they answer, "For the buffalo."

"But there are no more."

"No, we know it."

"Then why are you going on such a foolish chase?"

"Oh, we always go at this time; maybe we shall find some."

Index

Abilene, 131; exploiting buffalo, 150-151
Adobe Walls, how built, 187; used by hunters, 188; battle of, 189-192
Alexis, Grand Duke, of Russia, visiting the West, 146-147
Alvarado, Hernando de, expedition into buffalo range, 15
Ambush, Indians hunting from, 19
American Bison Society, 229-231
American Fur Company, 90, 94, 95-103
Apache Indians, 16; culture-origin tale, 1; horsemanship of, 24; in battle of Adobe Walls, 189
Arapahoe Indians. *See* Cheyenne.
Aricara Indians, in fur trade, 87
Arkansas River, hunters' "dead line," 185-186
Arms, ammunition and, 133, 217; outfit for sportsmen, 143; for professional hunters, 159, 160-161
Arrows, Indian skill with, 44-45, 146
Assiniboine, steamboat, 98
Assiniboine Indians, bartering for robes, 85; in fur trade, 87; *piskun* hunt, 37
Astor, John Jacob, 95
Atchison, Topeka and Santa Fe Railroad, in "Royal Gorge War," 199-200; volume of buffalo bones carried by, 222

Baker, I. G., robe buyer, 204
Banff, buffalo preserve at, 228
Bannock Indians, bartering robes, 85
Bates, Mr., furrier, 152
Baynes, Ernest Harold, work toward preservation, 229-230
Bent, William, 187
Berkeley, Grantley, on buffalo as food, 110-111
Binneteau, Father, 26
Blackfeet, 30, 219; chief's dress, 29; in fur trade, 86, 87; *piskun* hunt, 35-36, 37
Boone, Captain, on bull boats, 111-112
Bows, of buffalo bone and horn, 29
Brackett, Lieutenant-Colonel, 179
Bradbury, John, on herd behavior in rutting season, 7
Brunot, Felix, Commissioner, in land treaties, 172, 207
Buffalo, habits and characteristics, 3-8; mired and drowned in streams, 6, 71, 113; fights between, 7, 9-11, stampedes, 107-108, 121-122; vital spot of, 164-165. *See* Captures, Descriptions, Extermination, Food, Hair, Hides, Pemmican, Preservation, Robes, Rutting season, Slaughter, *passim.*